An Autobiography of Survival

Dr. Richard C. Kuendig

First edition

Published by:

Adverbage, Ltd.
New Ross,
Co. Wexford,
Republic of Ireland.

First printing: 2003.
Printed in the United States of America.
ISBN 0-9541723-2-9

Contents

To my wife and best friend, Miran,
and to my mother and father

Foreword

My mother died when I was in my thirties. By then, a long and difficult path had led me to where I am today; enjoying a wonderful life with my wife Miran, and maintaining a successful practice as a psychologist. I am sure that Mom never expected to see me succeed. During the long years of my childhood and adolescence, I was a constant source of anxiety, torment and pain to her. So much so that, after a particularly unpleasant family feud that I had created she actually told me she wished that I had never been born, and then despised herself for feeling that way about one of her own children.

I would give anything to be able to take back all the heartache I caused, but I know that I cannot. I can only give thanks that I was allowed to make things right during her lifetime and tell her how sorry I am that I could not have been a better son.

When Mom was dying of lung cancer in the hospital, I held her hand and apologized for having been such a difficult son for so many years. I knew that this would be my last chance to try to make amends and I had asked my family for a few precious moments alone with her. Mom squeezed my hand back and told me that I had more than compensated in adulthood for all the problems I had caused during my youth. She had never stopped loving me, even though doing so had not always come easy. Words are not adequate to describe that moment, and it is not easy even to write about, years later. I loved my mother deeply and I know that my eventual survival of the grip that

ADHD had on my life and any successes I have enjoyed are due in large part to her.

I have been lucky. The love and support of my family and wife, the help of God and, I must admit, a healthy portion of my own stubbornness have enabled me to build a successful life on the shaky foundations of a troubled youth. Most people with ADHD, Attention Deficit Hyperactivity Disorder, are less fortunate.

As a person who has the misfortune of having ADHD (and, believe me, it is an enormous misfortune), and as a clinical psychologist who specializes in the treatment of the same, I invite you on a journey from personal tragedy to learning how to deal with the effects of this so often misunderstood condition.

This book has been written to help readers understand the true nature of Attention Deficit Hyperactivity Disorder from the perspective of someone who has the disorder and has had to carry this burden for a lifetime. Some of the following pages will be based on what we know of the science of ADHD, but the emphasis is always on the individual experience of the disability which destroys so many lives. This is my story of growing up with ADHD. It allows the reader to "get inside the skin" of someone who has ADHD and has survived the horrible impact of the disability, as well as showing the point of view of a psychologist who specializes in the treatment of this monumental and far-reaching developmental disability. Although the name of the condition is well known – almost as a cliché or byword – public ignorance of the pain, the self-questioning, the constant accusations and the realities of living with ADHD remains considerable. Most people simply have no idea what it is like to have ADHD, and to live with this extra burden for a lifetime – a lifetime potentially full of misery, misunderstanding and the need to defend oneself simply to maintain a minimal sense of self worth while never seeming to achieve anything of any significance. The public has no way of knowing that many of the actions of someone with ADHD are caused by the condition itself, which propels them to act first and think later. As an ADHD child, I used to toss the cat into the pool, and feel sorry for him later, and drag my little sister into games which were too advanced for her, without thinking about her feelings. Those who do not have ADHD tend to assume that apparent carelessness or chaotic behaviors represent deliberate choices, because public ignorance is such that they just do not know any better.

People with ADHD are alternately feted for their spontaneity and liveliness, and punished for their heedlessness and lack of thought and consideration. It is hard for them to grow up with a "normal" set of criteria and learned responses to the cultural, social and professional environments in which they find themselves.

Countless hours of my childhood and adolescence were spent crying in my room, because I just could not understand why other people did not see the world the way I did. Without any understanding that there was something wrong with me, my experience of life was that it was a hostile, unwelcoming place with incomprehensible rules and harsh punishments every time one of those rules was broken. I was not diagnosed as having ADHD until I was in my mid-thirties. The realization was a great relief. At last, I understood that my feeling of not being fully in control was accurate, and it wasn't my fault. For the first time, I was able to begin accepting myself for who I am and consciously instigating ways of managing my own behavior.

I first started to write this book over ten years ago. I think I may have completed two or three pages. Revisiting the project over the years was similarly unfruitful. Like many people with ADHD, I find it difficult to stick to a long-term project and follow it through. The fact that I've finally managed to do it truly indicates the commitment I have to the messages contained in these pages. As someone with the condition, I understand the pain that ADHD can cause, and I know that there are literally millions of people in the world going through the agony that has damaged me and those around me from early childhood.

Much of the grief undergone by people with ADHD is caused by general ignorance of the disorder and total failure on the part of parents, teachers and the public at large to come to terms and deal with it. ADHD is a developmental disorder that causes those with the condition to experience the world very differently to those without it. ADHD sufferers are *literally unable* to think before acting. If this book serves to change the life of even one single ADHD sufferer, or to enhance the tolerance of just one of the members of their family, it will have fulfilled its purpose.

Is ADHD a disability or a handicap? The difference lies in the way in which people with ADHD are treated. The person who cannot walk is only handicapped when they are in an environment that is not conducive to living in a wheelchair. When they are in a home adapted to the needs of wheelchair users, they are still disabled – but they are not handicapped. Similarly, the person with ADHD has a disability, but is handicapped only when nothing is done to adapt his living conditions to the disability. The disability, therefore, belongs to the individual, while the handicap is owned by the environment. This small difference frequently forms the crux of the horrors and tortures faced by a person with ADHD throughout a lifetime.

I want to make it clear that this book has been written specifically from my perspective; that of a person with ADHD. At no point do I wish to say anything negative about the many people who have played a role in my life. When I refer to the impact that their behavior had on me, I am making a point about public ignorance of ADHD and all it entails, and not suggesting that anyone had a deliberate intent to harm me. On the contrary. Most of the people you will meet in the pages that follow are mentioned because I know that they loved me, and that this love pushed them to do things that they thought were right. Things they thought that I needed to help me to overcome my impulsive behavior. Unfortunately, their efforts were fuelled by their ignorance of the problem that we were all dealing with. This lack of information was the factor that hurt everyone involved, and not free will or intent on anybody's part. I suppose this is abundantly clear when I look back at the night I had to apologize to my mother before she died. This dreadful night was one of the worst of my life. I knew that I had to talk to Mom about the many things that I had done, and that I knew had been experienced as hurtful by my parents. I knew I would never have the chance to do so again. As I sat on Mom's bed, she was barely able to breathe the pure oxygen that she had been provided with. Taking her frail hand in mine, I said, "Mom, do you remember the night in New Hampshire when I knocked you down?" Her eyes filled with tears and I could feel her trying to squeeze my hand back as she smiled at me in affirmation. I had almost wished that she would have forgotten. "I'm sorry for hurting you, Mom," I told her. "I never wanted to do that." We had cried together before, but this time was different. This time, the tears we shared spoke of understanding as we both cried because we loved each other and not because we were experiencing emotional pain. "I know, Richard," Mom told me. "You have made up for that night a thousand times over." When we hugged each other for the last time before she was gone forever, we both understood that all her effort and anger, and all of the pain we both bore in our relationship was the result of ADHD and was, finally, a thing of the past.

Richard C. Kuendig, Psy.D.

1
What is it really like?

> *" ... society holds widespread and deeply seated beliefs about the nature of self-control and moral conduct. Its members are quick to morally judge those who may fall short of the mark and behave in less than responsible fashion."* – Russell A. Barkley, ADHD and the Nature of Self-Control.

"I hate you!" I used to scream at Mom and Dad as a little boy, when things had gone wrong for me, yet again. But what I really meant was that I hated *myself*. Boy, did I hate myself. Even more than I thought that my parents hated me.

I cannot remember a time before living with the certainty that I was a bad seed. The only stupid, clumsy dummy in a family of bright, high-achieving kids. When I was punished for misbehaving (and this happened often), the message I received was that I had been born evil. I was sure that nothing I could do would make Mom and Dad love me the way they loved their other children. I knew despair long before I was old enough to understand the word.

It took me years to become able to stop thinking of myself as a failure and a loser. Throughout all of my incarnations – as Dick the troublesome, fearful child, Dick the wild, long-haired, popular-with-girls teen, Richard the psychology student who still liked to party as if he were a teenager and Richard the clinical psychologist and husband – I could always hear a sneering voice commenting on my performance: "You think you're cool? You're not! You're just fooling them, and sooner or later they'll find out!"

When I was a little boy, I worried that my parents would get so angry that one day they would just decide to get rid of me.

The Kuendigs as children with Mom. I'm the little one on the right with the wicked grin

As a grown man, I still have not managed to free myself of the fear that my wife will do exactly the same. A part of me still "knows" that I am bad, and that I do not deserve to be loved. By and large, I have come to accept myself the way I am, but that little voice has never completely left me, and it probably never will. A part of me will always despise myself for having ADHD. For not being the "better person" I was always supposed to be, or at least the person I was always told I should have been.

My conviction that I was a flawed person has been shared by many of the people in my life, including some of those who loved me the most. My father never quite managed to stop seeing me that way. Years ago, when Dad lost a roll of silver dollars he had bought as a collector's item, he was convinced that I, an eight year old trouble-maker, had stolen them. I had not. I *had* done plenty of other things to aggravate and upset him over the years, but stealing those coins was not one of them. He never accepted my plea of innocence. Just a year before he died, Dad said, "Richard, I *know* that you took those silver dollars." By then, I was a practicing psychologist with a successful business and, after years of strife, I'd grown very close to Mom and Dad. But do you think he believed me? Of course not, he believed my history as a troublemaker! The loss of those silver dollars had been preying on his mind for thirty years or more, and once again he wanted me to admit my culpability and take my punishment. Dad was never able to let go of something that bothered him, and he did not find it easy to admit when he was wrong. In fact, I don't remember him *ever* doing so! The irony is that, as a psychologist, I can give Dad a retrospective diagnosis of ADHD, too. The chaos that has so often ruled my life and threatened to destroy my attempts to attain happiness also ruled his, as he went from job to job, state to state, and unreasonable outburst to unreasonable outburst (such as the time he accidentally dropped a bucket of paint on poor Mom when he was working on a ladder – and then blamed her for being in the way).

In their different ways, all of the Kuendig children loved their father, but none of us would claim that he was always an easy person to get along with. I think that my relationship with him was the most conflictive of all. Perhaps it was hard for him to look at me and see himself and the challenges that he also found so difficult. If my diagnosis of ADHD came late in life, he was left alone to deal with his difficulties by himself until the day he died and, like anyone else in the same situation, he did so imperfectly. I am sorry that I was not more understanding of him when I was growing up, but I was like him, caught in the grip of ADHD and the self-indulgence it facilitates or creates.

People with ADHD are difficult to deal with. They are hard on everybody else, and they are especially hard on themselves, even if they do seem to be nothing more than hedonistic fun-seekers. Too many internalize the feeling held by others that they are incorrigibly flawed, deficient, disposable people with little to offer society. Too many are never diagnosed and offered the help they need. Too many are abandoned to inadequate educational systems and parental support networks and grow up to become unsocialized, unqualified, problematic and emotionally erratic adults. Too many spend their lives hurting themselves and others, endlessly apologizing for their actions in the hope that the apology will dismiss the behavior that caused the pain as if it were a bad dream that never happened. But it did. And it will not go away. Ever.

ADHD is a developmental disability without a cure, but there are many ways in which it can be treated to minimize the harm caused to the individual with the condition and to those around them. With the right help, people with ADHD *can* hold down good jobs, succeed in academia, business and family life, and be happy, useful, fulfilled people. Without it, too many spiral out of control, and become attracted to alcohol, drugs and

This is my Dad. His calm expression in this photograph hardly reflects reality!

other forms of destructive behavior at the cost of personal and family happiness. During my own lifetime with ADHD, I have seen both sides of the equation. I can never be complacent about the condition, as I have been homeless, destitute and strongly attracted to drugs and self-destructive behavior. But I have also managed to become a successful professional and ADHD has had its part to play there, too.

ADHD, Attention Deficit Hyperactivity Disorder, is a condition present from early childhood (and, nowadays, usually diagnosed at this time). It is demonstrated by a range of behavioral traits, especially strong tendencies towards inattention, the inability to gather information from the environment through one of the five senses, impulsivity, the tendency to react to environmental distractions so quickly that there is no time to "apply the brakes", the inability to maintain effort and persist with an activity over time, and generally acting without thinking. In most (if not all) cases, the condition is still present, albeit in a somewhat modified form, in adolescence and adulthood.

Some adolescents and adults who were not diagnosed as children experience relief – as I did – on realizing that problems they may have experienced all their lives were due to ADHD, and not a personal flaw or character deficit, as they have come or been led to believe. Others are outraged at the suggestion that there is something wrong with them, and insist on continuing to believe that the world is the problem, not them. Sadly, the latter frequently never seek the help they need and continue to live as angry, embittered men and women who rarely attain their intellectual or emotional potential. Chances are, most of us know at least one person who fits into this category ("I don't know why John never got on in life" "She's her own worst enemy" "He just does not want to succeed").

ADHD influences a large number of children in the United States – as many as between 5 to 14% – and, if untreated, can lead to severe stress for the child, their families, teachers and classmates. We have all known a child who has seemed impossible to control, teetering wildly between unrestrained joy and bitter defiance. I was that child; you may have been too. ADHD is not an uncommon condition.

Various theories for the origin of the disease are under discussion, but it seems probable that there is a strong genetic element. In other words, if you or your child has ADHD, it is not your fault, or theirs.

ADHD is a very real condition that has to be managed for as long as the individual in question lives, and remember, this is something that effects not only them, but also their whole family. Life presents many challenges to us all, and even people with no neurological disturbances or health problems can sometimes find it overwhelmingly difficult. This simple truth is multiplied a thousand times in the case of the person suffering with ADHD.

A diagnosis of Attention Deficit Hyperactivity Disorder can be both devastating and confusing for the parent of the child so classified, for the child himself and for the adult sufferer. What exactly does the term mean? What will the outcome be? Is there a cure? Do treatments work? Should medication be prescribed or not? Am I crazy? Am I sick? Do I have to tell my classmates/teachers/colleagues/friends? All of these issues will be discussed in the chapters that follow, but let us get started by taking a quick look at the history of the diagnosis, and the various treatments that have been attempted over the years.

Prior to the identification and diagnosis of ADHD, children displaying the above behaviors were generally dismissed as being, quite simply, bad. Parents and educators alike accused them of *refusing* to listen, *deciding* to disobey and *neglecting* to think of others. Pastors and spiritual leaders accused them of succumbing to temptation and some even tried to exorcize the demons that they thought were inhabiting their restless bodies. They were expelled from school, ostracized by their communities and sent to prison with no psychological treatment whatsoever. When they died from accidents caused by reckless behavior or substance abuse, made desperate pleas for help in the form of suicide attempts or wound up old, bitter and alone, searching for happiness at the bottom of a liquor bottle, they were held exclusively to blame. This attitude had tragic consequences for too many lives to count. We have to know the past to understand the present, but we must not *stay* in the past. It is time to move on because if we let yesterday rule today, tomorrow will always be difficult.

Ignoring the condition or, worse still, punishing it, had and continues to have little or no positive effect on the sufferers in childhood, who frequently progress to develop further problems in adolescence and adulthood, resulting in deep personal distress and often serious harm to themselves and/or others. Behind many successful and failed suicide attempts lies a case of ADHD, diagnosed or undiagnosed. And where there is ADHD, there is usually a lonely, isolated individual who has never been able to hold back tears of shame for what they believe to be their personal shortcomings.

Fortunately, many of the children with ADHD are now identified, although members of certain ethnic groups are more likely to be untreated than others.

The medical community formally acknowledged Attention Deficit Disorder, as it was then known, in 1980, when it was included in the American Psychiatric Association's *Diagnostic and Statistical Manual of Mental Disorders* for the first time. The term was modified to include the word "hyperactivity" in 1987. Prior to the 1980s, the condition was variously referred to as "hyperactivity," "hyperkineticism," "hyperactive impulse disorder," "hyperactive child syndrome;" "developmental hyperactivity," "hyper-kinetic syndrome," "minimal brain dysfunction," "minimal brain damage syndrome," "moral control deficit," and "organic drivenness," if it were acknowledged at all, and not dismissed as mere "badness", a desire to be the classroom clown, or general unruliness. Most parents, not to mention health practitioners, knew nothing of the disability and how to manage it. From my own experience, I know that Mom and Dad struggled to understand why I could not conform to the family model of high achievement. "Why can't you be more like your brothers?" they often yelled, when I had disgraced myself yet again. It was not a rhetorical question, and I wanted to know the answer just as much as they did: "Why can't I be more like them? When Bill and Dave decide to play ball, Dad is pleased with them. When I do, I always end up breaking a window and getting into trouble! And when I tried to make cookies as a surprise for Mom and Dad, they yelled at me for getting the kitchen in a mess, even though they are always happy when Libby cooks ..."

Despite the fact that widespread recognition of the condition is relatively recent, it is in no way new. ADHD is not a modern phenomenon, and it is unrelated to recent cultural developments, changes in diet or modern methods of child-rearing. Regardless of what certain "authorities" claim, it is not caused simply by drinking too many sodas or consuming foods with additives. I wish it was.

Today, ADHD represents the most common reason behind a child's referral for psychological treatment. Public awareness, although not always well-informed, is considerable, partly because of greater education in the public sector, and partly because of intensive marketing on the part of pharmaceutical companies, who wish to insure that their drug sales increase along with the frequency of the diagnosis (more on that later).

Those who doubt that ADHD is not merely a recent phenomenon should be referred to the scholar, physician and scientist Hippocrates, who wrote 2500 years ago that there are some people who have " ... *quickened responses to sensory experi-*

ence, but also less tenaciousness because the soul moves on quickly to the next impression"[1] – an excellent description of the condition. ADHD has always been with us. It always will be. Deal with it.

[1] From Hippocrates: Aphorisms. In *The Genuine Works of Hippocrates* (Translated from Greek by Francis Adams).

2
"Mommy, why am I so bad?"

When I was a little boy, and I asked this question, my parents were not able to answer me. They made some suggestions, though: "Because you don't pay attention," "Because you don't do your homework," "Because you like to make your little sister cry," "Because ..." But none of their responses ever came close to answering my question. I needed to know not *what* I was doing wrong, but *why* I was not able to stop doing it, no matter how hard I tried.

Many children with ADHD are still treated as if they really were bad, and not suffering from a disability, but thankfully we know a lot more today that we used to and at least some of them are given the help they need to grow into successful adults.

Regardless of what some media figures claim, a diagnosis of ADHD is not given lightly when the individual in question

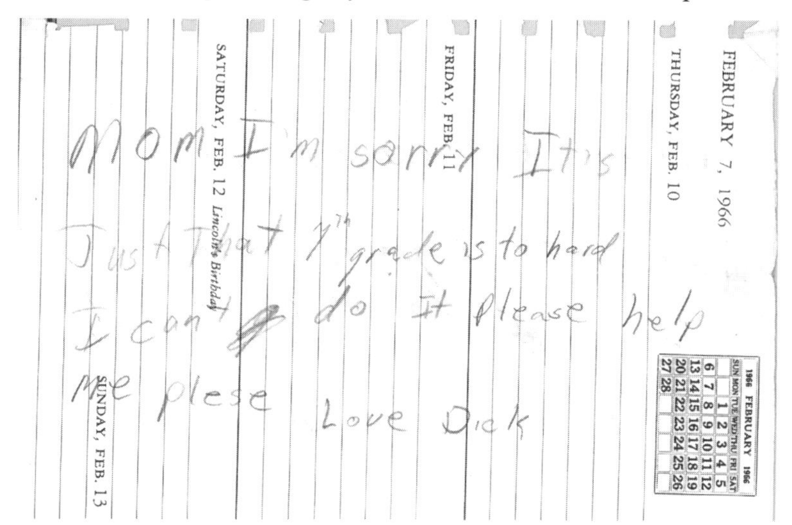

The handwriting looks like that of a much younger child, but I penned this miserable cry for help in seventh grade.

sees a responsible health practitioner or psychologist. Parents and teachers may feel sure that there is something wrong with a child, and refer him or her to a doctor, but it can be difficult to make a positive diagnosis in a clinical situation. Often, children (and even adults) are overwhelmed into silence by their surroundings, and do not behave the way they usually do.

Only by discussing symptoms in detail, and looking at issues such as family background and incidence of the condition and by determining whether there is an underlying learning disability can the physician, psychiatrist or psychologist make a positive assessment. My professional experience has shown me that one should be cautious of *any* diagnosis that is made in a single visit to a physician's or even a neurologist's office. The unfortunate reality is that our society has placed a huge responsibility on medical doctors to make a very difficult diagnosis after a brief office visit. ADHD is not a condition that presents with immediately obvious symptoms, like a rash or swelling.

It has been estimated that a thorough diagnosis of ADHD requires close to two clinical hours per patient, a luxury not many physicians have. Above all, no clinician can give a diagnosis of ADHD without considerable input from parents and teachers, and a positive diagnosis is only made if the relevant symptoms are present for a period of not less than six months prior to the age of seven.

But we are still left with the question "Why am I bad?" We are a lot closer to the answer than ever before, but a definitive response is still elusive. It is likely that, in the future, brain morphology may provide further diagnostic evidence, as we know that there are certain differences between the brains of people with ADHD and those without the condition.

Everyone's brain is divided into two sides, known as the left and the right hemispheres. The brain is divided into four lobes, which control motor activity and feeling. Thought is controlled by the frontal lobe, and this is the area which contributes to the presence or absence of ADHD in the individual. It has been demonstrated that people who have suffered damage to the frontal lobe as a result of injury to the head often exhibit symptoms similar to those of ADHD, and all the research points to the problem lying here – a flaw in the complex neurological structure of the frontal lobe, and the chemical transmitters that carry messages between the various sections of the brain. However, a great deal of research needs to be carried out before a definitive diagnosis can be made using neurological techniques. We do, however, have access to a range of therapeutic approaches which can greatly help the individual with ADHD in managing the condition. Our responsibility at present is to ensure that these approaches are implemented.

The only truthful answer to the question, "Why am I bad?" is, "You are not bad. You have a disability. We are not 100% sure what causes it, but we can help you to learn how to manage it."

3
Being a kid with ADHD

"Let me see if Philip can
Be a little gentleman;
Let me see if he is able
To sit still for once at the table."
Thus Papa bade Phil behave;
And Mama looked very grave.
But Fidgety Phil,
He won't sit still;
He wriggles,
And giggles,
And then, I declare,
Swings backwards and forwards,
And tilts up his chair,
Just like any rocking horse--
"Philip! I am getting cross!"
See the naughty, restless child
Growing still more rude and wild,
Till his chair falls over quite.
Philip screams with all his might,
Catches at the cloth, but then
That makes matters worse again.
Down upon the ground they fall,
Glasses, plates, knives, forks and all.
How Mama did fret and frown,
When she saw them tumbling down!
And Papa made such a face!
Philip is in sad disgrace . . .[2]

Kuendig family lore relates that of my mother's six children, I was the only one that caused problems from the very beginning. While my brothers' and sister's births went smoothly, Mom was very sick and in pain when I came into the world.

"Dick was trouble from the very start," she used to say, as if my destiny had been mapped out for me as a newborn, or as though I, as a tiny baby, had willfully made life as difficult

---

[2] Hoffman, Heinrich, *The Story of Fidgety Phil*, Struwelpeter, 1863. Hoffman was a German physician who left us a series of poems about wayward and difficult children in the form of a collection of verse. Many consider "Fidgety Phil" to represent one of the earliest clinical descriptions of ADHD.

as possible for my mother and those around me just as she thought I did later on.

The anecdote was supposed to be funny, but as a child painfully aware of being different – although unable to verbalize what those differences might be – and of causing difficulties for Mom and Dad despite my earnest efforts not to do so, it really hurt. Like many children in similar circumstances, I became sure that I had been unwanted and was living on borrowed time. I thought that Mom and Dad regretted having had me, and only put up with me because they had to. My attempts to please them always went wrong and my clumsy apologies were misunderstood and often seen as manipulative efforts to escape punishment.

For as far back as I can remember, I was always the impetuous one, the careless one, the lazy one, and the one who would do anything for a laugh, regardless of the consequences. The idea that my character was an unchanging, unchangeable quality was embedded in my sense of self. I knew that I was bad, that I had "come out wrong". And although it was not really true, I "knew" that, as a result, Mom and Dad loved me less than they loved the others: "Of course they don't care about me. I'm nothing but trouble. I've heard so often enough."

Now, I can see that Mom and Dad did not really love me any less. I may have been harder to *like* on a daily basis, but, without backup and support, Mom and Dad did love me and did try to help with the limited tools then at their disposal. There was no concept at that time of a developmental disability that made apparently healthy children "badly behaved." They had no idea why I was unable to listen, to sit still, and to learn how to succeed at school and on the ball field. In fact, they thought I was failing because I wouldn't try hard enough. They were sure that I would be happier if I could do those things and, in an attempt to help, admonished me whenever I did not succeed.

My earliest memories are from the age of two and a half or so, when the family relocated (a frequent occurrence throughout my childhood because Dad was *always* changing jobs after falling out with employers or employees yet again). The contents of our house were being loaded into a moving truck, and I recall the sheer panic of seeing the only world with which I was familiar being dismantled. Panic turned to outrage when attention was turned to my room and my furniture and toys were packed for transportation. As the men carried my bed away I yelled, “No, no, boys. Dickie’s night-night.” The men laughed, and Mom picked me up and carried me inside.

A lot of my early memories are about things that went wrong – my own misdeeds, being frightened by my surroundings, failing to understand what was going on, and just not getting along with anyone in authority, from the kindergarten teacher who pinned me to a chair so hard that my arms hurt while she screamed in my face that I just had to stop running around, to my own parents and elder brothers, who all seemed to be in a constant state of frustration with my unruliness.

I *wanted* to be good, to be liked, but no matter how hard I tried; I was never able to accomplish it. I was as clumsy as a young puppy, so eager to be accepted that I always ended up knocking things over, breaking precious objects, and getting in the way. I always tried too hard to please, and this made my already awkward attempts even more prone to failure.

“Just get out of the kitchen,” Mom yelled when I tried to help her make cookies and tipped the flour out all over the floor. “I have enough work to do without you making a mess!”

“Go away!” the other children told me when I tried to join in their game. “The last time you played we all got in trouble because of the broken window. Go and play with somebody who likes you.”

“Put that down!” my father told me sharply, when I tried to carry his newspaper over to him. “I’ve had a long day and the last thing I need is you crumpling up the paper before I have even had a chance to read it."

"Get out of my room!" all my siblings told me. "We don't want to see you. You always ruin *everything*. And *stay out of my stuff*."

Eventually, the string of rejections ground me down and I got upset, angry and frustrated, lashing out at whoever or whatever was around ("It's not fair!") and fulfilling the idea that everyone had of me as a troublesome character.

On the other hand, life also involved the constant pursuit of pleasure, at almost any cost. I was full of ideas for great things to do, and whenever I had an impulse, I acted on it straight away. My younger sister Libby is still disgusted by the habit I developed of plucking wings and legs off bugs so that I could watch them walking round and round in circles. So far as she was concerned, I was torturing them. For me, it was just an amusing way to spend a few minutes before hurling myself headlong into another activity. Did I stop to consider that bugs, lowly as they are, are living creatures that experience pain? No, I did not. No bug was important enough to come between me and my fun (my own self-preservation was only marginally more developed than my environmental sensibilities).

My desire to enjoy life was stronger than any sense of a need to avoid danger, too. One Sunday, when the family was on its way to church in Dad's Chrysler 500, I decided that it would be cool to use the speed we were cruising at to parachute myself out of the vehicle. Out I flew! Panic … the car screeched to a halt and my parents leapt out.

"Dickie! Are you all right? Can you move? Where does it hurt?" I could see the pale, anxious faces of my siblings pressed against the car windows and wondered why they looked so upset.

I was bleeding, and hurt, but more than prepared to do it all over again (I guess this reckless behavior can be seen as a predictor of my later turmoil). When Mom and Dad's concerned faces peered down at me, I laughed gleefully back at them instead of crying.

"Look! I'm bleeding! Did I look like Superman? Did you see me flying? Did you see? Can I do it again …" A strong hand grabbed me by the arm and pulled me upright and, if I am not mistaken, Dad uttered a few words he would not usually have used in front of a child.

Mom patched me up, and installed me in the front seat of the car, where she fondly imagined I wouldn't get up to trouble. She looked away for a moment, I reached across her and opened the door and – Mom flew out! Oh boy – that was fun (for me)!

I was four years old, and it is safe to say that I was already considered "quite a handful". Things didn't get any easier as I got older. I must have been seven or eight when I couldn't tear myself away from playing with my brothers for long enough to visit the bathroom (I have to confess, even now I hate interrupting anything to go the bathroom. It seems like *such* a waste of time). I waited, and waited, and eventually the inevitable happened. I pooped in my pants. *Not* smart, not at all. But I literally couldn't bring myself to leave the game. My next priority was to hide what I'd done from my Mom, so I hid the dirty pants in the medicine cabinet in the bathroom. You can imagine how long it took for her to find them. A Freudian would probably see a hidden message in my action – I think I just didn't sit still long enough to think it through.

Even when I was still tiny, Mom and Dad dealt with my unruly behavior at the beach by fencing in our picnic table, and leaving me caged inside, under the table, with nowhere to go. An appropriate way to deal with an ADHD child? Definitely not. But understanding of the condition at that time was far less even than today, and I expect they felt themselves to be at the end of their rope. They were probably afraid that I would do something to hurt myself or one of the other children, that I would swim out of my depth, disappear or turn up causing trouble at the farthest end of the beach. And, in all honesty, it is possible that something of the sort could have happened. ADHD children are notoriously accident-prone and are often called clumsy. But remember that people with ADHD act before they think. Weighing the consequences of my behaviors before doing something was not likely to happen.

I am the first to admit that I was not easy to deal with as a child. Admonishments and instructions were literally in one ear and out the other, as I followed my first instinct every time, never stopping to think about the outcome of what I was about to do, because I could not. My mind worked on overtime; new ideas occurred to me more quickly than I was able to realize them and I spent my time starting to do fun things that, more often than not, I bored of before I had seen them through.

Half way up a tree, I would start thinking about how it would be great to be on the *other* side of the yard, playing with the family dog, so I would change tack. But before I reached my intended destination, I had changed my mind again and was on my way to the kitchen to break some eggs and make cookies, but then – "How about TV? Where are my brothers? What is that silly little sister of mine doing? Am I missing something crucial? Might it be even more fun to be somewhere else? Oh look! A butterfly is trapped inside the window, let's see if I can catch it …"

It is not surprising that my parents often despaired, but the person who suffered most as a result of my ADHD was myself. All children have their demons, but the ADHD child is unable to process these fears and rationalize them in any way. He or she feels them, and reacts immediately and without thought. As a small boy, I was terrified of so many things. My inner life was ruled by fear – fear of the dark, of monsters, of being punished … no sooner had a potential threat occurred to me than I reacted to it as if it was really there, at that very moment … *MOM!* My mind had raced ahead, showing me not only the dreadful face of the evil man in the wardrobe I shared with my older brother, but also the terrible, awful things he was going to do to us and the chaos and destruction he would leave behind when he was done. Oh no!

My inability to deal with emotion caused me to react with screams and cries instead of more thought-out requests for reassurance and comfort. When I was scared, I would go and sleep with one of my siblings. My older brother Herb grudgingly let me into his bed, but had a rule: "Not until I'm asleep". Anxiously, I fidgeted in the upper bunk: "Are you asleep yet? Are you asleep yet? *Are you asleep yet?*" I knew that I was not safe until I was tucked into bed beside him. My younger sister Libby would let me lie on the end of her bed, but never get under the blankets. Sometimes, I retreated to the floor next to her bed so that she would not kick me out of her room altogether, a thought that I found truly terrifying. As the little one of the family, Libby must have enjoyed the feeling of having power over an older brother, and believe me, she played it for all that it was worth. Any child would.

Like most kids in similar circumstances, my siblings also knew how to take advantage of my fearfulness and they did not hesitate to enjoy themselves at my expense. I recall one night going up to my room with the family pet, Squire, a small terrier, when the dog started barking furiously in the direction of the space under my bed, confirming all my fears that there really *was* some hideous monster lurking there, waiting for a juicy little boy to happen his way. As I realized all this, I could already hear the crunch of my bones breaking, and see the blood spread across the floor … Screaming, I ran to get my mother, who duly came upstairs to investigate and tell me, as she had countless times before, that there was nothing there and that I should stop wasting time and *go to bed.* Monster nothing! It was my brother Herb. Do adults forget how cruel healthy, normal children can be? I guess they must.

My older brother John played a more benign role in dealing with the panic I experienced at school, being called out of class to come and comfort me whenever I became hysterical and frantic, something he remembers happening often (I use the term panic advisedly. ADHD is an inability to inhibit behavior, and school frightened me because of the continuous onslaught of reprimands I was exposed to every day. Because I was unable to control my reactions, normal apprehension was expressed as panic).

It is important to understand that, while ADHD children do not have different fears to other kids, they are unable to control their reactions to those feelings of distress and anguish, and experience being frightened much more profoundly than their peers. They do not have a built-in safety mechanism that allows them to analyze the experience, rationalize it, and react with calm. They react as soon as they feel the fear, and the emotional paralysis that this causes prevents them from processing the information and experience in any meaningful way.

A major result of being frightened so much of the time was that, as a child, I was unable to enjoy anything wholeheartedly. My life was dedicated to the pursuit of pure pleasure, but that eluded me constantly. Quite literally, I do not remember any unadulterated joy from my early years. If I was not knocking things over, being clumsy and getting things wrong, I was worrying about doing so, or panicking about some less rational preoccupation. Just as I could not control my relentless pursuit of pleasure, nor could I ignore the knowledge that, sooner or later (probably sooner) I was going to be in trouble all over again.

As well as having to deal with psychological and behavioral issues, as an ADHD child I had the typical problems with fine motor control that plague kids with the condition, making it difficult for them to achieve good results in sports, writing, artwork and more. In America, where it seems that every little boy is on a baseball team, this was very stressful for me. Our little boys are not expected to have weaknesses but to strive towards being small men, instead of children. Their fathers encourage them to be tough, to be manly, to make the grade, to catch the ball … and make them feel useless when they are not able to. I could not play baseball, no matter how hard I tried, but my Dad was determined that I should be on a team and he found one for me and "sorted me out" according to the way he felt things should be.

By buying uniforms for all the boys on the team, Dad had been able to persuade the coach to take me on. That he did this out of love, according to his lights, is without question. I was a boy, wasn't I? I was his son, right? Well then, it was clearly my responsibility to prove my mettle on the field, and Dad was showing me how much he cared by making that possible. He came home that day with a smile that stretched from ear to ear.

"Dickie," he called. "Come and say thanks to your old man. I have great news. You're on the team!"

"Dad," I complained. "You know I hate baseball. You know I'm no good at it. Do I have to …"

Dad's face darkened. "You ungrateful little wretch. Do you know how much money I had to spend to get you on the team? You don't appreciate anything I do for you, do you? Well, you can just go to your room and stay there until you are ready to come down and say thank-you."

Miserably, I trailed up to my room, muttering angrily. Dad just did not understand me at all.

"He *know*s I can't play baseball," I reasoned. "He must want me to look stupid. Why can't he just let me do the things *I* like?"

Downstairs, Dad was just as upset as I was. He had thought that I would be happy, and that he had bought me the precious gift of acceptance by my peers. He had expected me to be excited. To give him a grateful hug. He had hoped that learning to play ball would make me more confident, assist me in developing social skills and give me the opportunity to make friends.

Boy, was he wrong.

My baseball career was a disaster. Playing ball did not make me feel more manly, or help me to be part of the team; it made it painfully clear to me and to everybody else that I was in the wrong place. Who was I kidding? I could not play ball and everybody knew it. I remember playing right field one day, standing and hoping that the ball would not come my way while I distracted myself by watching ants crawl in the cropped grass, and the wild flowers blow in the breeze, when someone hit it in my direction. My gaze was lifted from the fascinating sight of the ants carrying crumbs in and out of the entrance to the colony by the roar of the crowd to the horrifying sight of the white ball hurtling through the blue sky. Towards me.

"Oh no!" I remember thinking. "What am I going to do? This stinks!" Hopelessly, I stuck my glove in the air and … watched as the ball soared past me and thudded on the grass. My teammates were disgusted, and calculated their jeers to wound as much as possible.

"Oh no! He did it again! I *knew* that that would happen. Do we *have* to have that guy on the team? He's such a loser!" "Did you know that he is only here because his Dad paid for the uniforms?"

With athletic prowess at such a dismal level, I was always the last kid picked for a team. In fact, team captains would argue about who would have to have me on their team, while I squirmed with misery and embarrassment, "I don't want him – you take him!" "Coach, we had Dickie last time. It's not fair. It's their turn today." There was not a derogatory or hurtful name I was not called.

Maybe it is easy to laugh and dismiss a child's problems from the lofty heights of adulthood, but to the little boy or girl who is regularly tormented by their peers, pint-size tormentors are truly frightening, and every experience of being bullied is horrific.

My parents might have been able to help if they had had some understanding of ADHD and how it works, but like all parents and most child specialists in those days they did not. Instead, they unwittingly collaborated with the rest of the world in making my disability into a handicap, by insisting I change my behavior without giving me the resources to do so. If I wrote my homework messily, they said, "Write neater! Go and do it again," as if the only thing preventing me from doing so was my own unwillingness to cooperate. Hardly the best solution for a child experiencing difficulty with fine motor coordination and control. I was endlessly punished for not writing neatly. I became increasingly frustrated, and quickly learned to associate schoolwork with nothing but misery and humiliation, as Mom and Dad grew steadily angrier at what they saw as my stubborn refusal to really make an effort. They may as well have been yelling at a deaf child for not paying attention, and we all came away from the experience emotionally bruised, angry and confused. As you can imagine, having one very angry, upset little boy and two grown-ups at the end of their rope in the house did not help with the dynamics of the whole family in any way and my unmet emotional needs also interfered with my parents' ability to tend to the rest of their offspring.

Many adults with ADHD, diagnosed and undiagnosed, remain bitter about the way in which their childhoods were blighted by other people's inability to understand them, and their own inability to experience the world the way others do. It does not take a doctorate in psychology to understand that a child's experiences go a long way towards forming the adult he will become. When curiosity is met with punishments, and experimentation with parental rage, a child is on course to become an angry, frustrated adolescent, with all that entails, and an adult operating way below his aptitude levels.

I do not feel bitter about my past any longer, but what makes me angry today is that fact that, despite decades of research into the causes and treatment of ADHD, millions of children are still treated with the same level of ignorance that made it hard for my parents to help me and ended up damaging me and our entire family, and millions of parents are left on their own to cope with the sort of "problem child" who, untreated, can threaten the psychological well-being of every member of their family and, in the worst of cases, become a dangerous, violent adult later on.

Popular levels of understanding of ADHD are in no way consistent with all the advances of science and psychology. Why does our society persist in condemning ADHD children to unhappy childhoods, and to the likelihood that they will never achieve all they might? If my descriptions of an ADHD childhood help even one Mom or Dad to reassess the way in which they deal with their ADHD child, then all the effort expended on this book will not have been wasted.

4
"I think your child may have ADHD ..."

We have already discussed the warning signs of ADHD – difficulty in concentrating, impulsive behavior and problems with staying still. Parents and teachers may suspect that something is wrong for some time before a diagnosis is made – after all, they are the people who spend the most time with the afflicted child. If a child who is obviously bright is not obtaining good results in school and tends to be disruptive, for example, it may be suggested that he or she be assessed to see if ADHD can be identified. However, parents and teachers are not qualified to provide clinical diagnoses, and one should always be cautious of the teacher who suggests that a child needs medication without recommending that he see a properly qualified professional. No teacher, no matter how well-meaning, has the training to allow him or her to suggest medication.

A definitive diagnosis can be enormously stressful for parents, especially those who are not informed about the condition. They may wonder if it is their fault in any way, if their child has a viable future, and whether the problem will affect the whole family in a negative fashion. To be honest, it is possible

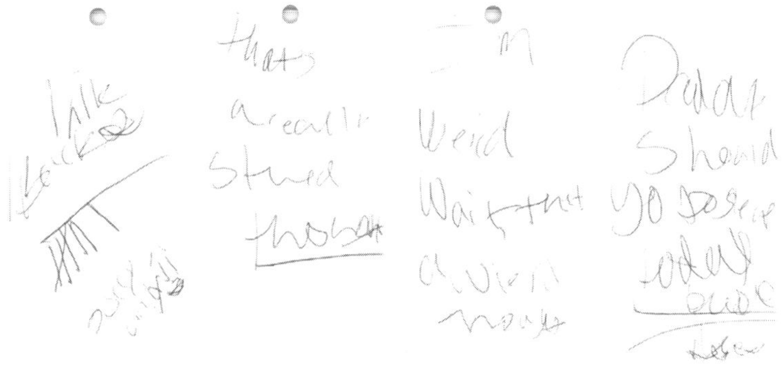

Diary of a young girl with ADHD

that suffering from ADHD will have a profoundly destructive impact on the individual's life – as it did on mine- and even on the entire family dynamic, *but it does not have to*, and therein lies the central message of this book.

When parents, educators and caregivers are armed with the proper knowledge, and a reliable professional cares for the child, he or she can overcome or compensate for the problem and develop into a successful, responsible adult. Seen in this light, the diagnosis of ADHD in a child who is habitually defiant or disruptive is news that is not so tragic; the condition has been identified and parents, health providers and educators alike can start working together to enhance the child's capabilities and help him or her work at modifying disruptive behavioral patterns. I am sure that if my family had been aware of ADHD and the various means one can use to enhance a child's behavior and the quality of his life, things would have been easier for us all.

We have already discussed the fact that ADHD is characterized by inattention, hyperactivity and impulsivity. What does this mean, in practical terms? While the child may find it impossible to concentrate on tasks that he finds uninteresting, absorbing, exciting activities such as video games may pose no problem. Impulsive behavior consists of acting without thinking – blurting out an inappropriate remark, rushing into the street without checking to see if a car is coming, or being unable to sit still in class. Some of the children I see on a clinical basis manifest all of these symptoms at the same time! I have equipped my office with a unit for playing video games so that, if they need to focus for a while, they can.

Problems of behavioral disregulation can magnify or illuminate a learning disability and cause difficulty in completing tasks well within the individual's abilities as well as problems with social relationships, friendships and family interaction. The child himself may realize on many levels that there is something wrong, and experience feelings of being "different" from the other children in his class or family, without being able to verbalize these troubling emotions. This can further heighten emotional distress, and cause him to "act out" his feelings of pain, mistrust and betrayal, making him even more defiant than usual. In my case, a large part of my problem was the misconceptions of other people, and in this I was typical of the ADHD sufferer. Most people look at the ADHD child or adult, and see someone with no obvious disability. They reason that they seem to be fine, they have ten fingers and ten toes, they can talk, they don't look disabled, and therefore they should be able to control or change their behavior. But they cannot, or at least not for every long, and this is what classifies ADHD as a disability.

ADHD is not the result of a deliberate decision to misbehave, it is a neurologically-based inability to think before acting. Many children, like me, have never known what it is like to be able to consistently look before leaping. This point must be understood before the condition can be addressed and treated in the case of any given individual. Insisting that Johnny or Jane sit down and pay attention is not going to work until they have been taught how to overcome their problems in doing so. You might as well scream at a deaf person that all they have to do is *listen*, for God's sake, or yell at the amputee that it is past time he learned to stand on his own two feet. Do not think that I am exaggerating here. These analogies are taken directly from the way in which people with ADHD are treated.

Children who have ADHD are at elevated risk for having a range of associated disorders, or co-morbid conditions. Learning disabilities, many of which are also thought to be related to subtle abnormalities in the brain, are more frequent with ADHD, including delayed development of speech and language skills, dyslexia or difficulty reading and writing and dyscalculia or difficulty in grasping mathematical concepts. All of these disorders can also coexist. Having ADHD makes successful treatment of a learning disability more difficult, as it is hard for the child to concentrate on the task at hand. As always, early diagnosis and prompt treatment of disabilities maximizes their likelihood of success. Many children with ADHD have average or above-average intellectual abilities and with the right support can be successful at school and in later academic pursuits, as I eventually came to be.

Anxiety disorder (the problem that caused me to over-react terribly to my fears) is thought to be due to both biological and environmental factors. Strong prevalence of the disorder in family members of an affected individual points to a genetic factor while in the case of the ADHD child especially, constant pressure, criticism and feelings of inadequacy, uselessness and a sense of being a "bad person" are certainly strong contributory factors predisposing the individual to the development of an anxiety disorder based on psychological stressors.

Although a wide variety of disorders can coexist with ADHD, and may be causally related, the treatment of the ADHD is not always enough to right the secondary problem. Parents and caregivers must recognize that language or other disorders will frequently require a different treatment approach and may not respond positively to the drugs used to treat ADHD. As always, patience and a managed, clinical approach go a thousand times further to righting a problem than frustration, punishments and bitterness.

Tourette's syndrome is a tic disorder characterized by the presence of one or more tics, such as involuntary movements, twitches, winks, etc., or by involuntary utterances, often of inappropriate words or phrases. The stereotypical sufferer of Tourette's syndrome is the person who curses and swears uncontrollably, and unfortunately, people with ADHD are at risk for having this problem, as if they did not already have enough to deal with! For a time, it was thought that medications used to treat ADHD could cause Tourette's syndrome, but now it is clear that while they may aggravate an existing, but undiagnosed, case of the disorder, they cannot cause it. By the way, one of the professors I had in graduate school used to refer to Tourette's disorder as "ADHD with tics," illustrating the close similarity of the two very different problems.

It can be hard to distinguish between ADHD and Oppositional Defiant Disorder. The two conditions can coexist in the same child, too, making the equation even more complex. ODD is not likely to be caused by genetic or biological factors, but probably results from the child's environment. In my case, I gradually developed a full-blown (and very unpleasant) case of ODD as a result of living with an untreated disability. In children with ADHD, the condition results from the way in which adults in authority deal with the child's failure to live up to their expectations of how he should behave. A close estimate is that approximately 65% of children with ADHD will eventually develop Oppositional Defiant Disorder. This makes perfect sense, as if a child with ADHD is managed by exposure to anger and harsh, inconsistent punishment and/or harsh parent/child interaction, he or she will learn that type of behavior. Remember, too, that many children with ADHD also have a parent with ADHD. As well as their genetic inheritance, the behavioral model they are presented with is a chaotic one. As the child uses anger-based behaviors to manage his own environment, the angry parent tends to reciprocate and a cycle has been established. The fact is that children with ADHD lack behavioral inhibition. When they react with anger, it is often unleashed with disproportionate vigor, making matters even worse.

A child with conduct disorder which is likely to be a worsening developmental progression of Oppositional Defiant Disorder can seem impossible to deal with. I know I was. Because of the bad reputation as an angry, over-active child I quickly acquired, I was always blamed when things went wrong, whether or not I was actually guilty. Under these circumstances, it was hard to keep respecting adult authority the way I was told I must. Grown-ups' fallibility and the ease with which they blamed the "usual suspect" (me) gave me little incentive to strive for approval. ODD is not just a diagnosis of the affected child, but of the entire family dynamic.

In my professional capacity, I see many children and young people with ODD, and I have no illusions about them – they can be downright unpleasant and, in extreme cases, even dangerous to themselves and others. However, in order for the ODD to become manageable or disappear altogether, the root causes of the condition – the interaction patterns within the family – need to be addressed. As well as providing the ADHD child with the treatment he needs, the entire family dynamic must be explored and dealt with. For many parents, this is hard to come to grips with, because in order to short-circuit the ODD family interaction style, they often have to take a very painful, close look at their own anger and how it impacts their parenting style. As a parent, one might feel quite justified in feelings of anger towards the child with ADHD, as did my Mom and Dad. But that sense of justification simply does not negate the impact it has on the developing child with ADHD or the evolving family pattern of behavior. Consequently, until the underlying family dynamic of anger and resentment is recognized and eliminated or at least minimized, the progression toward an ever-worsening psychiatric disorder is probably inevitable.

Many problems combine in the child or adult individual with ADHD, because of genetic factors, the psychological problems that can result from untreated or poorly treated ADHD, or both of the above. Impairments in memory occur to varying degrees in people with ADHD, and are probably caused by neurological shortcomings. Short-term memory is particularly problematic, causing or aggravating numerous daily routines and responsibilities as items to be remembered or tasks to be carried out are simply forgotten. Problems with cognitive processing show in difficulties planning ahead, anticipating problems, understanding and recognizing patterns and interpreting subtle behavioral signals given by others. All of this, combined with difficulty in sequencing, or enacting behaviors in an appropriate order, exacerbates difficulties that the child or adult is experiencing at school, in the workplace or in social settings. Difficulties in modulating emotional responses cause individuals to express whatever they are feeling times one hundred. Anger, upset, excitement ... all are demonstrated lavishly, to the point of disturbing whoever happens to be around. Difficulty controlling motor skills results in extravagant gestures, clumsiness and general boisterousness. One should not forget that the person with ADHD is likely to simply forget what they were about to do because the current moment will almost always erase the planning of some other mundane task assigned to them. Yes, it often does appear that the person with ADHD "intentionally" leaves things out of their assigned task but, more likely than not, they simply were overtaken by the moment and the here and now won over the need to remain on task.

Sleep disorders are not unique to individuals with ADHD, but individuals with ADHD often (but not always) have difficulty sleeping or awaking from sleep in the morning. In short, they seem to have only two speeds, "on" and "off", and switching from one to the other can take some time. The reasons for this vary, but are usually related to the ADHD sufferer's "constantly active" brain, their instinctive, knee-jerk reaction to fears and nightmares, a biological clock which is at odds with the time frame followed by society and other factors integral to the condition. My own problems sleeping as a child were clearly strongly related to the fact that I reacted vigorously and immediately to the fears that plagued me. I was unable to take the time to rationalize my worries and deal with them. I tried to cope with difficulties sleeping by snuggling up with my siblings, whenever they let me. In the mornings, I was usually sluggish, and took a long time getting up to speed.

Children who have been diagnosed with ADHD may, strange as it seems, benefit from having noise in their room, such as music or repetitive recordings of sounds such as rainfall, which block out distractions and allow their busy brains to rest. Medication to cause or enhance sleepiness is also available, of course, but it should go without saying that children should be medicated only when other methods have proven inadequate, so please be sure to try other, non-medical methods before you turn to medication, as our society has taught us to do.

Nocturnal enuresis is the technical term for bed-wetting, a condition which affects a large number of children with ADHD, even into the teens, and which can be the cause of great embarrassment and misery for the child – not to mention the inconvenience it entails for parents. Stated simply, enuresis is a failure to wake up when the bladder is full, resulting in the individual's urinating while he sleeps. It has been hypothesized that, in some cases at least, this may be due to the neurological dysfunction that lies at the root of ADHD. Anxiety disorders can also cause the condition. Children who suffer from late bed-wetting want more than anything to get better, and punishing them will not help. It might even make the condition worse, as it is bound to increase anxiety levels. One system that has been shown to be more effective in long term remediation than medication is that of installing a special alarm in the child's bed or underwear, which will go off when wetness is detected. With time and persistence, the child will become conditioned to wake when his bladder is full. Unfortunately, in many cases this treatment is discontinued before it has finished, causing a relapse of the troublesome behavior.

The research is quite clear that, although pharmacological treatments are effective, enuresis usually returns when the medication is withdrawn. Overwhelmingly, the use of behavior modification has been shown to be superior to medication (usually DDAVP) in terminating bedwetting and preventing relapse.

A problem associated with nocturnal enuresis is pant wetting during the day, or diurnal enuresis. Assuming that the child has all of his or her plumbing attached correctly, most children with ADHD who have this problem are simply too preoccupied with the wonders of the world that surrounds them to attend to such petty issues as visiting the bathroom. One can only hold one's urine in for so long before it has to come out! Children with ADHD who wet their pants seem, quite simply, too bored with the process of what they are doing to attend to their bodily needs. Nature eventually forces the issue.

Many children with ADHD suffer from encopresis, or a failure to manage bowel movements. You have already read my story of having an "accident" as a child when I chose to keep playing instead of visiting the bathroom. For a hyperactive child, the thought of having to leave what he is doing to visit the bathroom may be just too tedious to contemplate, and he will often decide to "hold on" to his bowel contents and keep playing instead. As time passes, he will either defecate unintentionally, causing himself deep embarrassment and distress, or will become severely constipated, as his body reabsorbs water from the stool which becomes hard and difficult to pass. If the latter occurs, laxatives or even an enema may become necessary. Chronic constipation will cause the child to associate bowel movements with pain, and generate extra anxiety around visiting the bathroom.

Problems with language occur so frequently among kids with ADHD that it seems likely that there is a strong biogenetic link. One of the most common aspects of ADHD is the tendency to act before thinking, and this also translates into the arenas of speaking and listening. The ADHD child or adult's thoughts race through their mind and erupt in sudden, unplanned behavior, or as a torrent of words. A difficulty in synchronizing thought and speech can cause individuals to speak so quickly that the words are garbled, not to be able to speak at all, or to stammer or stutter so that they are difficult to understand and can become embarrassed by their incoherence and inability to say out loud the words and phrases that they can say mentally with no problem at all. Of course, psychological factors play a role too. From an early age, many ADHD children have internalized the message that they are bad people, and find it difficult to express themselves because of the risk of getting into trouble all over again. "If I say what I think," the reasoning goes, "Mom and Dad will probably get mad with me, so I'd better not say anything at all." Language disorders might improve with medication, or with other methods used for treating ADHD, but additional treatment may also be necessary. Be that as it may, one must be aware that, for the individual with ADHD, what is private thought becomes public speech. In fact, I predict that, in the future, one of the foremost differential diagnostic symptoms of ADHD will be verbal overproduction. For now, parents and teachers alike would be well advised that to complain of "motor mouth" is tantamount to complaining about one of the core symptoms of ADHD. Put another way, they should learn to ignore the overly talkative nature of the ADHD individual, because that is one of the symptoms that is probably not going to go away.

Bipolar disorder, widely known as manic depression, is an increasingly frequent diagnosis in children who manifest symptoms generally consistent with a diagnosis of ADHD. One good and very likely reason for this may be that insurance companies cover treatment for bipolar disorder, while they will not pay for the treatment of ADHD. Solid criteria for determining bipolar disorder in children do not exist; psychiatrists extrapolate from their experience with adults with the condition and, to be truthful, many of the children so diagnosed may well have ADHD with or without other complicating factors and would benefit more from treatment for that condition than for bipolar disorder. It would be interesting to see if the same number of diagnoses of bipolar disorder were issued if doctors and parents were confident that treatment for ADHD was covered by insurance, but as things stand it seems that some children with disabilities are more equal than others. Do I sound cynical? Well, I *am* cynical. Years of living with ADHD, and working with children who have the condition have taught me to be so. I do not want to be a cynic but, at this point, I really see no other choice.

Because ADHD is most commonly diagnosed in childhood, this is when the issue of medication usually arises for the first time. For this reason, this is an apt point at which to include a discussion of the various treatment procedures available and what you should bear in mind if you have to decide whether or not to medicate your child. This book is not intended to be a complete guide to treatment with medication, however. If your child has ADHD and your doctor suggests medication, insist on discussing the pros and cons of the treatment in detail, as well as additional and/or alternative approaches that might be effective. Deciding whether or not to use medication to treat ADHD, or any disability, is something that must always be considered with great care.

Medication for ADHD has received a great deal of attention from the media in recent years, much of it negative and largely uninformed. While it is widely known that the prescription drug Ritalin is used in the treatment of children (and adults) with ADHD, the public is less familiar with how the drug works, why it is prescribed, and what the benefits of taking it are. Unfortunately, much public knowledge comes from the rather aggressive marketing techniques of certain manufacturers of drugs intended to control ADHD and similar disorders – *not* the most objective and reliable of sources! Another "fount" of information are the media, which tend to present ADHD and its treatment with medication in entirely unrealistic terms, suggesting that drugs are physically addictive and that all doctors and psychologists are unscrupulous persons who are only interested in lining their own pockets and are often unofficially in the pay of the pharmaceutical industry. Individuals with ADHD and parents of children with the condition find themselves caught between two strongly held and mutually exclusive viewpoints. One which tells them that drug treatment is wonderful, and alone holds the key to a bright future, and another which tells them that it is dreadful, won't cure the problem and will cause new and horrifying ailments. Sadly, many people find it difficult to access a reasoned analysis of the situation, cannot come to terms with the issue, do not trust themselves to make an educated decision about medication, and end up being swayed by one of the two incompatible viewpoints. In the real world, nothing is ever simple and this truth applies just as much to medicating ADHD as it does to anything else. Medication can be a blessing, and can change some people's lives unambiguously for the better – or it can cause more problems than it cures. Patience, reason and open-mindedness are crucial.

Let us not be unclear about medication – it works. ADHD is probably a neurological condition and drugs such as Ritalin and Dexedrine, specially designed to enhance the availability of neurotransmitters on the presynaptic neurons, can be extremely effective, especially in the short-term. The two major symptoms of ADHD, hyperactivity/impulsivity and inattention, both respond well to medication. Impulsivity and hyperactivity are probably controlled by dopamine, while inattention results from dysfunction in the cortex and mesocrotex of the brain. Low doses of stimulants work on the cortex and improve attention, while higher doses cause improvement with problems of impulsivity, etc.

In the afterglow of seeing a disruptive, unmanageable child become easy to handle, parents and teachers may heave sighs of relief and feel that the problem is effectively over. Little

Johnny is no longer disrupting the entire class at school, or causing headaches for the whole family every single night. He seems happier, too, and is achieving better results with his homework and school examinations. Why, there just does not seem to be any reason why Johnny should not do well if he takes medication for the rest of his life! However, any physician should think long and hard before writing a prescription. Medication for ADHD treats the symptoms, not the problem. It can be an excellent short-term answer to a problem, but is not always a viable long-term solution. If it is not accompanied by family therapy, behavior modification techniques and positive reinforcement, the problem will still be there when the medication is withdrawn or when the patient becomes reluctant to take it, as happens about 90% of the time in adolescence. Not all children are as happy about taking the drug as their relieved teachers feel, either. Some report feeling depressed, emotionally flat and anxious. Furthermore, there are often unpleasant side effects; loss of appetite, intolerance of medication, dizziness, anger, hair loss (alopecia), an exacerbation of a previously unidentified tic disorder such as Tourette's syndrome, rashes and more.[3] Research on the topic of the metabolism of medication in children is still lacking – growing bodies do not react to medication in the same way as adult ones, and my experience has shown that children under the age of five have much more difficulty in processing drugs than their older counterparts. It has been demonstrated that tiny, pre-school children with ADHD or ADHD behaviors do not respond as well to medication as their older counterparts. Any decision to prescribe medication should only be made *after* a detailed,

[3] A more comprehensive list would read as follows: Growth suppression, seizures, dependency and abuse, arrythmia, leukopenia, thrombocytopenic purpura, toxix psychosis, exacerbation of Tourette's syndrome, Erythmea nultiform, hepatotixicity, nervousness, insomnia, rebound, abdominal pain, anorexia, motor tics, headache, palpitations, dizziness, blurred vision, tachycardia, weight loss, fever, depression, angina, rash, urticaria, changes in blood pressure and cardio myopathy. Please note that not all medications carry identical side effects.

objective cost-benefit analysis. It should never, in my humble opinion, be the first step taken in addressing the problem and drugs should certainly never, ever be given before a diagnosis has been confirmed. Regrettably, some doctors do prescribe Ritalin and other medicines to children with suspected ADHD, "to see if they respond". An improvement in the child's behavior in these circumstances is thought to mean that the drug is acting on their brains, but, be careful, it does not necessarily prove a diagnosis of ADHD. The verified effect of the drug on the brain of the ADHD individual is mistakenly thought to verify the presence of the condition. Nothing could be further from the truth. Stimulant medications work in exactly the same way on all human brains, and the fact that a person with ADHD responds to the medication simply means that they actually took the medicine. These medications are not diagnostic in any way at all, and if your doctor claims that a positive response to them means anything, run away! Psychotropic medications such as Ritalin are often prescribed by family physicians, who do not have any specific training in the identification and treatment of ADHD. The fact that disturbed children often react favorably to the drug confirms the propriety of the treatment in their eyes. Aggressive promotion to medical professionals and parents of drugs designed to treat ADHD also blurs the issue, presenting potential benefits of the drugs in an entirely unambivalent light, while ignoring risks and possible alternatives. This is irresponsible in the extreme.

Medication should *never* be taken lightly. When dealing with disruptive ADHD children, the pros and cons need to be carefully weighed before coming to any decision about writing a prescription. How severe is this child's behavior? Will medication just dull the symptoms, or will it allow parents, caregivers and educators to initiate techniques designed to help the child to maximize her or her abilities? Is the diagnosis of ADHD certain – has care been taken to rule out other causes of the disruptive behavior? Has the family dynamic been explored?

ADHD-like symptoms can sometimes be caused by emotional, rather than neurological, disturbance. Will the benefits of medicating the child outweigh the side effects and the drug's limitations? Are parents and caregivers looking for a quick fix, or will the medication be just one part of a holistic treatment and management plan? No decision should be made until all of these questions have been answered satisfactorily. As a clinical psychologist formally trained in psychopharmacology, I do see children whom I feel need medication, but because taking drugs to treat ADHD is a long-term treatment strategy, I don't take medicating my clients lightly. Only about 40% need to take prescription drugs, and I stay within those parameters. In general, our society devotes far too much attention to seeking a quick fix to any given problem. With ADHD, much to the chagrin of the insurance companies, *there is no quick fix*. Parents, teachers and caregivers must recognize that they need to make a long-term commitment to the ADHD child if he is to become an adult whose behavioral problems are satisfactorily managed. ADHD is there for life. Intelligent parents will read the literature currently available about the drugs prescribed to their children, but they must remember that studies are often biased. Pro-drug studies look for, and find, beneficial effects. Anti-drug studies do the opposite!

ADHD can be treated either by stimulant medication or by a wide variety of medications, although stimulants are the drugs most commonly employed. In my experience, as I state above, approximately 40% of children with ADHD should be medicated and although many professionals would heartily disagree with this statement it is my opinion and I believe it warrants merit. In actuality, many more children are given drugs to control their condition, often with little or no other treatment. The fact that positive effects are usually seen in disruptive children (even those who do not have ADHD according to objective criteria) can cause family physicians, parents and teachers to rely too much on medication. It works, but it treats the symptoms, not the disorder itself. Medication should never, ever be the sole approach to managing ADHD which is *very often* the case in the classroom. We can compare this approach to the physician who doles out painkillers to the patient with abdominal pain, without looking into the reason for the pain.

Considering that so many children, adolescents and adults are considered to be hyperactive, the idea of treating these people with stimulants can seem bizarre: "Aren't they already stimulated more than enough, for Heaven's sake?"

Just how do stimulants work within the patient's brain to help with the symptoms of ADHD? One of the main causal factors of ADHD is a problem with the neurons in the brain, which may not function properly. Stimulant drugs help to release the reabsorption of dopamine and norepinephrine, two brain neurotransmitters, and they decrease inattention, distractibility, over activity and impulsivity in three quarters of individuals with AD/HD. However, when the stimulant medication is withdrawn, most of those individuals who have been treated with medication alone do not continue to manifest improved behavior, illustrating the point I make above – medication should represent part of a holistic treatment plan rather than the only treatment.

Anti-depressants can also work in treating the condition, although because a majority of patients with ADHD react favorably to stimulants, the latter are usually tried first, with anti-depressants used as a "second option", as the risk of suffering from side effects is, for many people, somewhat higher. Usually, anti-depressant treatment is attempted when stimulants have been used, and have failed, when the patient suffered adverse side-effects from stimulant medication or when the ADHD is accompanied by a co-morbid mood or anxiety disorder. However, 90% of patients over pre-school age prescribed stimulants do improve, although it may be necessary for them to try a number of drugs and dosages before arriving at exactly the right one for them. At the end of this book, you'll find some basic information about the various drug treatments available at the time of writing.

Punishing the child who has all or any of the above problems is less than ineffective, but there *are* treatments and behavior modification systems that can help and the sooner they are applied, the better. Difficulty in acquiring social skills, for example, is largely due to the ADHD individual's inability to stop and think before acting. Helping him to slow down, and showing him the positive benefits of struggling, and succeeding, at mastering basic social skills helps enormously. Patients who have been shown to require medication generally show great improvement in all areas once their medication regime has begun, with especially dramatic results in the area of motor skills. All of the above can be also helped with a comprehensive, consistent strategy of behavior modification and management.

Never forget that medication can help, but is not and must never be the only treatment provided. People with ADHD can learn how to help themselves without the need for a chemical crutch.

5
"We are family ..."

> "*You would cry and Mom would say you didn't have to do the chore, like the dishes or mowing. She would say you were too young, though the rest of us had to do more at the same age. You big baby, Mama's boy* ..." Bill Kuendig.

> "*I remember that you were always teasing me ... one thing you did that traumatized me was to give my favorite doll a mohawk.*" – Libby Kuendig.

I am from quite a large family – I have four older brothers, Bill, Dave, John and Herb and a younger sister, Libby – and I know from bitter experience and a desperately unhappy childhood that a child with ADHD changes the entire family dynamic. Libby was born when I was four years old and although I *never* deliberately mistreated her (yes, Libby), I did regard her as a plaything for many years. She, in turn, quickly learned that because I was often disruptive I was *always* blamed when things went wrong – even when problems were not my fault. Libby knew that just by screaming and blaming me, I would get in trouble – no questions asked! That knowledge must have been empowering for the smallest child, and only girl, in a family of brothers.

Of course, all children squabble and compete for parents' attention, but when ADHD is part of the equation, sibling rivalry acquires a whole new element, and both ADHD and non-ADHD children suffer as, of course, do the parents (not to mention the family pets, silverware, ceramics and harmonious relationships in general).

In fact, I *was* often unintentionally cruel to Libby, because I never stopped to think about the fact that she was younger and smaller than me, and did not necessarily want to take part in my boisterous games. I did not consider the fact that games I thought were fun often ended in Libby's tears. What Libby remembers as my victimization of her was me, the impulsive fun loving brother with ADHD, acting without even knowing I should have thought about those actions first. ADHD children live for the moment, and younger sisters and brothers are re-acted to without thinking. If an idea seems like fun, it is acted upon immediately, and the issue of whether other people are equally intrigued by the idea is moot. I often did things that people saw as being daring. When I was fourteen, I jumped off a fairly high cliff in the dead of night, not because I was particularly brave but because I didn't give it a second thought. If I had, there is no way I would have jumped. The fall was so long that about half way down I braced my legs for impact – and nothing happened. I just kept falling. When I did finally hit the ground (after what seemed like an eternity) I ended up with a minor injury to my right ankle.

If I gave little thought to the possibility of injuring myself, I did not give much more to the thought of other people being hurt when we played. "Let's play, Libby!" I would cry. "Come on, it'll be fun. Put down that stupid doll, who cares about a doll? Take my hand, let's run. Get up. What do you mean, I made you fall? Oh, come on, it's not bleeding *that* much. What do you mean, you'll tell Mom? Tell Mom what? I didn't make you fall! We were just playing. Is that Mom? She looks angry! I'm outta here …"

I span Libby into my action, without stopping to think about what she wanted, whether I might accidentally hurt or frighten her or whether my behavior was appropriate. The thought that Libby might not want to do the same things as me, or find the same games amusing, was irrelevant. I did not think about what Libby might like to do, and then do what I wanted anyway, I just did things without thinking at all! There just was not time to think. I picked Libby up, tossed her about, teased her and made her play the sidekick in whichever game I was currently involved in.

One of the most common social problems I encounter in my practice is the problem children with ADHD have in making and/or keeping friends. It is not uncommon at all for a child of almost any age to tell me that they do not have friends. When asked why not, the child will almost always say that they have no idea. One child I treated described himself as a "ghost" because his peers didn't want to have anything to do with him at all. The parents of these children, however, often tell an entirely different story, seeing them as intolerant, bossy or inflexible. Children with ADHD will often state that all they want to do is play with other children, but the other kids are not playing fair. In reality, because ADHD is an impulse control problem, the child probably changed the rules of the game midstream to ensure their victory. Then, when the peer protests, thwarting the goal of the ADHD child, he is met with strong opposition which is then interpreted as an unreasonable demand. Already, the relationship between the two children has begun to perish.

Readers who grew up with ADHD or with ADHD siblings are probably nodding their heads knowingly at this point. It is a familiar story. In my case, if an idea occurred to me, I acted upon it immediately. (*Come on! Let's play!*) It was too bad if my idea of fun was not the same as the other child's. In Libby's case, I do not think she ever learned to understand that few of the things I did were ever intentional. In fact, I know that she is still angry with me at times, for crimes committed when we were both barely ten years old. Perhaps I should say that her inner child is still really, really angry with mine …

Just as I used to toss the family cat in pool because I thought it was amusing without stopping to think about what the cat thought about the situation, I involved Libby in my games and intrigues, without ever being able to pause to wonder how she *felt*. Life was there to be lived at a hectic pace, and every idea was enacted straight away. How Libby responded to the activities I involved her in was entirely outside of my awareness. We were having fun. Weren't we?

All of my older brothers were good at sports – and I mean *good*. Mom and Dad were justifiably proud, we had home movies of their various triumphs, and their medals and trophies were on display. Of course, I wanted to be just like them – and of course, I was not. I was just the stupid little brother, tagging along and never managing to make the grade: "Go away, Dick. You'll just get in the way. Go and play house with Libby or something."

A kid with ADHD is just not cut out for the sort of concentration and applied effort necessary to succeed at long-distance running and I was woefully inadequate. I tried for a while, and I do remember my older brother Dave turning up to a race and urging me on as I came in, second to last: "Go, Dick! Don't let that last guy pass you." It meant a lot that he came because my parents, by then, had all but given up on believing I was going to do anything I said I was going to do and understandably, they didn't believe that I was going to run in a race at all. By that time, it seemed to me that the rest of the family had pretty much given up on me. I was the habitual loser. The also-ran. It was too bad that I had had the bad luck to have been born without intelligence and grace into a family of bright, gifted children. What was the point of hoping more of me than I was able to deliver? I had taught my family a powerful lesson over the previous years: "Dickie has lofty ideas, but he never follows through." My family had learned, at my tutelage, that they were justified in believing that my ideas were good, perhaps even grand, but that I wasn't going to finish them. Beginning new things was fun, but finishing them was a bore.

"What lovely boys," a lady beamed at Mom outside church. "I hear they've been taking home all the medals. And what does little Dickie do?" She reached out a gloved hand and patted me on the head.

Oh, Dickie ..." Mom said, her tone embarrassed. "Ah ... Dickie's our little butterfingers. He can't catch a ball. Can you, honey? We still haven't found out what Dickie's good at." The lady withdrew her gloved hand and smiled at me sympathetically. I thought about snapping at her fingers as they passed my face, but managed not to. "We still haven't found out what Dickie's good at ..." Mom had said. I knew what she meant: "Dickie isn't good at anything."

One should bear in mind that those of us with ADHD do not necessarily lack physical prowess and ability, but rather the ability to stay focused on those things that are considered boring. Lack of concentration lies at the absolute crux of our problems with organized sports.

I was not diagnosed as having ADHD as a child, but many children are today. Although this is a good thing, it does introduce some more issues for consideration. When a child is diagnosed as having ADHD, the effect reverberates throughout the whole family. While parents may be distraught or even relieved that the problem finally has a name, the impact on the child's siblings can be much more profound and complex. Frequently, brothers and sisters of a child with the condition react strongly and negatively. They may feel that their sibling is absorbing all of the time and attention of the parents, that all of his "bad" behavior is excused on the grounds of the condition, and that maybe they, too, should start being defiant in order to attract the same level of attention. Some children begin to deliberately misbehave in an attempt to receive the attention they feel is rightfully theirs, while others become withdrawn and introverted. Resentment is inevitable when one child damages or destroys another's toys, books, or artwork, and this sort of behavior is, unfortunately, typical of the ADHD child who acts first and thinks later. While adults can look ahead to a time when their ADHD child will have progressed to a much higher stage of self-control, it can be hard for children to look into the future, and those who experience family life as chaotic and unpredictable can assume that it will *always* be like this and learn to see the world as an unfair, unfriendly environment. In my case, Mom and Dad did not know that I had ADHD, and Libby certainly had no way of knowing that I did not really want to hurt her. None of us had any concept of things getting better, beyond the fact that, eventually, I would have to grow up and leave home.

While caring for an ADHD child can take up a great deal of any parent's time, it is important not to let the situation impact negatively on other children. If they are old enough to understand, explain the condition to them as clearly as you can. Make sure that they comprehend that, while their brother or sister might require some extra patience and understanding at times, he is not more loved, or more special in any way. Of course, they also need to realize that he is not *less* loved and special! It is important to be fair, and to be seen to be so, but it is also important to recognize that fairness does not necessarily involve treating children in exactly the same way. Chores and duties are harder for the ADHD child to fulfill, and must be tailored to meet their capabilities. One child may not be able to fulfill the responsibilities that another one could at the same age, and vice versa. Fairness is about giving everyone what they need, and treating everyone as they need to be treated. Remember, too, that with children, as with adults, emotional responses are rarely as complex as they seem. At one and the same time, siblings may love, hate, envy and despise each other.

Because of the genetic component of ADHD, sometimes more than one child in a family is diagnosed with the condition (I strongly suspect that one of my brothers also has ADHD, although he would probably not agree with me). In any case, as a psychologist I quite frequently encounter families struggling to cope with several children presenting with ADHD in a variety of ways. Needless to say, having two or more ADHD children in one household can be a recipe for extreme stress and tension for all involved. The disability affecting both children must be recognized, and treatment provided for each. However, the way in which ADHD manifests itself may not be identical, because of differences in age, gender, position in the family and personality type, not to mention the myriad of different ways in which parents interact with their various offspring. I am familiar with the case of two little girls – sisters – both of whom have ADHD. As is the case in most families, each child has adopted a role peculiar to herself. One is the "disruptive" child, and one is the "well-behaved" child. The roles have become so ingrained in their views of themselves that they are almost independent of the ways in which the children actually behave. These little girls' parents have fallen into the trap of seeing their daughters in these roles, too. This means that when Little-Miss-Well-Behaved is being boisterous and loud, her behavior is not experienced by them as problematic, while when Little-Miss-Disruptive is being relatively calm and good, she may yet be seen as misbehaving and unfairly chastised. It is important to learn how to see the reality of the situation, and not to react to arbitrary roles.

When a brother and a sister in the same family both have ADHD, there is often a danger that the boy will receive most of the attention – helpful and otherwise – as his behavior is more likely, on average, to be loud, disruptive and perhaps at times violent. Even if his sister is more disabled by the condition, she may risk being passed over if the foremost symptoms are an inability to pay attention and "connect" with other people (inattention is frequently the most noticeable effect of ADHD in little girls). Although she is at as much risk of being damaged by the condition as is her brother, her behavior is less disturbing to the adults in her life, and may not always be identified as problematic. This situation is unfair to both children, as the little boy is tagged as the "bad" child, and the little girl may not receive the treatment that she needs. The boy is placed at high risk of developing Oppositional Defiance Disorder and the little girl may never achieve the academic milestones she needs to make the most of her education and future career possibilities.

All parents of ADHD children know that there is an aggravated risk of their child becoming physically hurt as a direct or indirect result of the disability. The child who does not think before acting is the child who leaps from the top of the tallest tree in the yard with a Superman costume on, and breaks his arm, or the child who dashes out into traffic on her bicycle, and is involved in a traffic accident. When there are two or more children in the same household with similar behavioral problems, the risk that they will be physically injured is aggravated as they spur each other on, get angry, lash out at each other and compete: "You think you're so cool in your Superman costume? Just wait until you see me jump through *this* – after I've doused it in gasoline and set it on fire" or "You can jump from the garage window? Ha, that's nothing! I'm sure I can fly off the roof, and I'm going to show you how!"

While the ADHD child can feel less favored that his siblings, and thus "victimized" by the situation, brothers and sisters of children with ADHD can perceive themselves to be the victims of their unruly sibling, especially when they are younger. As was the case with me and Libby, ADHD kids tend to be so self-involved and occupied with the pursuit of pleasure that they often forget that what is fun for them is not fun for smaller, more vulnerable playmates. Their boisterousness can seem violent and uncaring, and result in the smaller child suffering from feelings of victimization, often fuelled by the fact that they do indeed get bruised and scratched in the course of vigorous, unwanted play. How can a small child possibly understand that their sibling does not intend to wound them when he damages their possessions, "ruins" their games and interrupts when they are trying to relate a story or an incident from school? They easily become prey to the conviction that their ADHD sibling's greatest pleasure in life is to bother them and to be involved in everything in the home all at the same time, that their parents either do not know or do not care, that there is little or nothing they can do about it and, lacking an adult's time perspective, that the problem is going to last *forever*. That they are *always* going to be smaller. That life is, by definition, all about being knocked over and trampled upon in the stampede that is their elder sibling's innocent notion of play. All of this is a lot to bear, and it is not surprising when profound anxiety is the result, along with the associated misbehavior and acting out, ranging from bed-wetting to defiance and anger.

How can these sensations of victimization and powerlessness be counteracted? First of all, if the child with ADHD is being properly treated, things will get better. He will gradually become more equipped to control his reactions and to stop and think before doing something. Until that time, parents may find it necessary to physically separate their children so as to ensure that accidents or unplanned mistreatment do not occur. If the child with ADHD receives favorable attention and praise when he makes a big effort to be kind to his younger sibling, this will help to reinforce the positive behavior. Effort needs to be expended to ensure that the child without ADHD knows that his good behavior is appreciated and that his support in the family and with his sibling's condition is noted and recognized. I remember trying really, really hard to play a game that Libby enjoyed, and even sitting down with her to dress and undress what I saw as her "stupid dolls". In reality, I did not care about the dolls. I wanted Mom to see that, sometimes, I could be good. I even called out to her, "Hey, Mom, look! Libby's doll can do karate!" For once, Libby was taking pleasure in my company, and I still remember that it felt really good to see her smile at me and feel that I was being seen as the kind older brother for a change. But Mom looked over at us playing on the floor and saw trouble waiting to happen. She rushed over and grabbed me by the arm, pulling me across the carpet.

"How many times have I told you not to mess with Libby's dolls?" she chastised me through clenched teeth. "Just get up to your room and stay there until I say that you can come down. I'm just glad I caught you before something terrible happened!"

As I left the room, I could see Libby looking after me, with confusion written all over her small face. This time, we had been having fun. But Dickie had still gotten into trouble. What did that mean? That Dickie was bad even when it seemed like he was being good? How confusing!

On the other hand, older children in the family can become resentful when they are put in a position of responsibility that they experience as unfair or onerous: "Don't let your brother get into trouble;" "Make sure that Jimmy takes his medication on time;" "If your brother gets over-excited, be sure to calm him down." If they are seen to fail in containing the behavior of the younger child, they may become extremely angry for being reprimanded for what is, after all, the "bad" behavior of someone else and to rail against the injustice of having to assume adult levels of responsibility while "everyone else" can go out, be an ordinary kid and just have fun. Parents should be wary of giving older siblings more responsibility that they are emotionally prepared for. It is important to let all the children in the family be children, not just the ADHD child. Children without ADHD should not be given responsibilities unsuited to their age and level of maturity. An atmosphere of resentment is not the right one in which to build positive relations between family members, and instead creates a situation in which bullying and intimidation are likely to flourish to the detriment of each and every child, including the one disabled with ADHD.

Siblings of children with ADHD may bitterly regret that their family and their brother or sister cannot be "just like everybody else." They may feel that the child with ADHD has somehow stolen the chance of a better or a perfect childhood from them, and even come to see the family as having experienced a profound loss with the birth of the affected child: "It's not fair. We used to be so happy, didn't we?" "Why did this have to happen to us?" "What did we do to deserve having someone like this in our family?" "If only Richard had never been born, we would be so happy together." They must be taught to understand that their sibling's problems can, and will, be overcome and that having a disability, or a family member with a disability, is not a valid reason for shame and sorrow. It certainly does not mean that their family is worse than any other family nor that their afflicted sibling can be blamed for every single thing that goes wrong.

It may be helpful for children to know and understand that many families have members with ADHD, and even worth joining a support group so that children and adults alike can intermingle with other people in the same situation and even complain to contemporaries who understand what they are going through. I'm sure that Libby would have benefited from being able to share her experience of being the younger sibling of a child who seemed to be willfully beyond control with another child in a similar situation.

An essential element of the treatment of a child with ADHD is the exploration of the family dynamic. It is well established that one child with ADHD can impact negatively on the whole family – but how can the family impact on the ADHD child? Damaging interactions can create and maintain a problem. One common perception of the ADHD child is that he is less loved than his siblings. He gets in trouble more, is yelled at more often and is subject to more disciplinary interventions. Often, a majority of his conversations with his parents center around his defective behavior and the negative impact it has on the family unit. It took me many years to realize that, although my relationship with my parents was very confrontational, they did not love me less than they did their other children. I was yelled at the most often, sent to my room more than anybody else, and frequently told what a pain I was, without being given help to overcome my difficulties with school and with my interactions with my siblings and other children. As a result, I had internalized feelings of inferiority from a very early age, along with the conviction that there was really little point in trying to be good, because I could not, no matter how much I wanted to.

Children's emotions are felt at least as strongly as adult ones, but a child's reasoning is less sophisticated and complex. If parents show a child, by their angry words and disciplinary actions, unaccompanied by positive reinforcement and tolerance, that he is a lesser being than his brothers and sisters, he will soon grow to understand, rightly or wrongly, that he is less loved. When I see children with ADHD in my office with their parents, I often hear them say, "Mom, you love him more than you love me ..." It is like listening to an echo from my own childhood, and I hurt for both parent and child, because I know what both are feeling and understand the frustration involved in the failure to communicate properly that marks so many parent-child interactions.

On the other hand, once ADHD has been identified and systems of behavior modification have been put in place, the siblings without the condition may become angry at what they see as the unfairness of their brother's reduced workload, and the special incentives he receives simply for behaving as they do all the time. "Why should I bother being good," they may feel, "when my brother is so bad, and never gets into trouble?" In these circumstances, there is always a risk that the disgruntled sibling will turn to self-destructive behavior, motivated not by a disability, but because he or she feels that the parents' attention is all focused on the ADHD child and that, to receive their care and time, it is necessary to misbehave. Parents must be careful to treat their children fairly, but fair treatment does not mean that all the children of a family should be considered to be exactly the same. Different children have different needs. Balancing these diverse needs and demands with the ordinary chores of living – careers, housework, simply making sure that there is a meal on the table when there should be and more – is not easy, and it does take all of the efforts of both parents to keep the family running smoothly. I would never dare to suggest that raising a family and administering a household while juggling work and finances was easy. But I do suggest that a realistic approach to the diverse needs of all the members of a family results in greater gains over time. When adjustments are made to the treatment of the child with ADHD, and to the changes that this causes in the lives of the other children, the family *will* begin to run more smoothly, and everyone will be happier and more productive.

Children learn much more by example than they do by following instructions, and the primary arena in which they form impressions of the world and their place in it is in the family. Small boys and girls look to their parents and to their siblings to understand who they are, what their purpose in life is and what will become of them as they grow older. To help children with ADHD to move beyond the disability and towards a well-rounded future, the family as a whole must function well, and irrational ideas about the whys and hows of life must not be allowed to develop.

It is difficult, but early investments of time and effort have enormous rewards later on, as parents see all of their children, disabled and otherwise, become able to reach their full social, academic, and emotional potential. I've said this before, but it is worth repeating; ADHD can destroy lives. But it does not have to.

DATE: October 18, 1965

DIVISION: 5A

Richard Kuendig is doing unsatisfactory work in arithmetic due to:

✓ Lack of attention

✓ Lack of knowledge of basic number facts

✓ Incomplete homework assignments

✓ Lack of study of material covered in the classroom

____ Frequent absenteeism

If you have any questions concerning this please contact the school.

SIGNED Mrs. Kuendig

I forged this signature to get myself out of trouble. Not surprisingly, I was caught!

6
School Days

> "*Weak... could do better if he tried*" – report card, typical child with ADHD.

For the child with ADHD, school can be a minefield of potential humiliations, disasters and misery. It certainly was for me. Even now, some memories of school can make me feel like a frightened, humiliated little boy, and the teachers of my past loom as large as the giants they really were when I was small.

First grade was a major challenge for me, and not one that I was able to meet. I had been so excited about starting school, of becoming the "big boy" that my older brothers were. Soon, I told myself, I would be able to read and write, and do math, and Mom and Dad would be really, really proud. It took my first grade teacher about a week to decide that I was more trouble than I was worth, and that the best thing she could do with me was try to keep me quiet so that the other children could work. I trailed behind my classmates, angry with myself for not being able to keep up, and frustrated because I knew I should be able to do the things they did.

"Dickie just isn't making progress at school," I overheard Mom telling Dad one night when they thought that I was safely in the den watching television.

"He'll be alright," Dad replied. "He's not stupid. He just needs to work harder."

I repeated. The end-of-year exams, which most likely focused on how to play with others without conflict, were too much for me. While I should have been bent over the page with my tongue protruding in concentration like all the other kids, I was watching the school janitor cut the grass outside the window, always so much more entertaining, or wondering which raindrop would be the first to trickle all the way down the glass and onto the ledge (the ability of those raindrops to race down the glass was simply a marvel). Or anything, really, that captured my attention more than the tedious chores that we were given. Besides, I found no use for all that academia anyway. I mean, what was I going to do with writing and reading – write a book?

"Well, Dickie," the teacher admonished me on the last day of my first year at school. "I hope you've learned your lesson. I hope you'll be a good boy and work hard next year so you won't have to watch your friends move on without you another time." My teacher made the classic mistake; she thought that the failure of this year was going to have an impact on me *next year*! I could not have cared less about next year. Next year was so very far away that it didn't even exist in my consciousness. In order for we ADHD folk to be influenced by the future, we have to pause our behavior long enough to recognize that the now will affect the tomorrow. Unfortunately, pausing my behavior was (is) not on my strong asset list. In fact, behavioral inhibition was (is) nearly nonexistent in my life. So when the teacher admonished me to work harder next year, I gave her the obligatory "yes I will' (with a certain dash of emotional somberness) in the hopes we could soon end the most boring conversation in existence so that I could get to the more important business of play and, well, more play.

I *had* learned my lesson. I had learned that, no matter how hard I tried to work and how much I struggled to fit in, I couldn't. And I had learned that it was all my fault, and that nobody would ever help me. They did not care. That was my fault, too, because I was a bad little boy.

Years later, when I realized that I had ADHD and discussed the past with my Mom, she didn't even remember that I'd repeated the year, and I had to go and dig out my old report cards to see that my memory was not at fault. Repeating the year was not a big deal to my mother or father, who thought they were doing the best thing for me. But my experience of that retention was very consistent with current research that demonstrates grade retention to be *far more harmful* than beneficial! For some reason, teachers and school, administrators have a false belief that retention is a good thing. Well, *retention is bad* in all respects. Did you know that retention in one grade increases the likelihood of quitting school by 50% and that 100% of the kids that are retained twice quit school? Not to mention the simple fact that 96% of kids that have been retained in one grade report the experience as being equally devastating to the trauma of a parent's death? I was no exception and my mother and father didn't even remember that I had been retained! The academic community should really rethink their ideas about retention and follow research which suggests that moving the challenged child on to the next grade and provide lots of remedial help so that he can catch up is a much better option.

My early failure has stayed with me always, as have the memories of the other first graders kicking me out of the sand box: "Get out of here, dummy! We don't want you!" "Go away! Miss, Dickie is spoiling everything …"

So far as they were concerned, no doubt, I was ruining their games. Perhaps I was being excessively rough, jostling my playmates. Or maybe I did not sit still long enough to listen to the rules of the game that they had invented. Quite likely, I kept interrupting the ringleader with ideas as to how we might improve upon the activities he suggested. Either way, as I understood it, the message was clear: "You are too stupid even to play with us. Go away. *We don't want you*."

I don't mean to imply that being shunned by others is a documented symptom of ADHD, but the problem I was immediately confronted with in the first grade was my inability to calmly play with other children. I had the best of intentions and wanted – desperately – to commune with my peers, but they seemed to do everything with agonizing slowness. I remember myself in first grade feeling an overwhelming need to experience everything at once. The new environment of the school presented me with unprecedented excitement and jubilation. There were new friends to be made, new toys to play with, and new people to talk to. On my first days at school, I was sure that my education was going to be a glorious experience. I could hardly contain my excitement as I burst into the class with unbridled happiness exploding from me like champagne from a shaken bottle. I thought that everyone was going to be my best friend. I *knew* that it would be wonderful.

My first acquaintance in school was Rick M. I caught sight of him playing with friends in the area where the wooden blocks were kept and, attracted by the bright colors, went to join in. With all the grace of a newborn pup, I blundered straight into the tower Rick had just finished building. What fun! I followed my impulse to dive headlong into the building blocks that poor Rick had spent so long piling one on top of the other. The blocks toppled over and fell to the ground with a clatter. I could not have been more pleased with the effect of my entry to the game. I had not given a moment of thought to the other little boy, and now I heard the screeching torrent of Rick and his friends lamenting as they formed their first opinion of me, their new classmate. At all of five years old, I was the great destroyer, the nuclear warhead of first grade fun.

"What's the problem?" I wondered. "This is such fun!" I invited Rick to help me to rebuild the tower of color, only to discover that he did not want to be my friend. My clumsy joy did not attract him. It made him mad.

As an ADHD child, learning the rules of juvenile society came quite easily. I have ADHD, I am not stupid. When, as a little boy, my peers treated me like the plague, I soon realized that something was wrong. But I could not worry too much about the morality of social behavior, because my hedonic nature would have been inhibited and that, of course, was an impossibility. In reality, I wanted more than anything to be part of the group, to be one of the popular kids. But because of my tendency to speak before listening, to act before thinking, I was never going to have the chance to become so. Such is the plight of any child with ADHD. Life is full of wonder, but nobody else seems to participate in it. Those of us who have ADHD have to try to cope with the curse of not being able (yes, *able*) to delay impulse gratification, to slow down our behavior long enough for our thoughts to guide us.

I often wonder what it would have been like to be patient rather than impulsive. The impulsivity of people like me must be equally foreign to anybody who does not have ADHD. The idea of behavior preceding thought must be an utterly alien concept. Remember that, to someone with ADHD, behavior preceding thought is both normal and natural, and when someone without ADHD thwarts our need to act out an impulse a state of internal tension is created, making us feel both bad and uncomfortable. The next problem, of course, is how to get rid of this unpleasant internal state, the frustration that external rules impose on us. Unfortunately, there really is no way for us to do so, and the ADHD child in particular does what comes naturally. He nags ceaselessly, or gets mad until something takes over the blank space left by the unmet impulse.

As a psychologist, I have had the occasion to speak to literally hundreds of parents of children with ADHD, and without exception they all make the same error of attribution. When their child starts to pester their parent, apparently without mercy, they are seen as being intentionally unpleasant:

"He seems to enjoy nothing as much as he *enjoys aggravating* his Dad."

"She is *never happy* until she has reduced her mother to tears."

"I've told him a thousand times that he won't get anywhere by nagging me, but he just *refuses to listen.*"

"She could make things a lot easier for herself if she would just pay attention to what I say, but she doesn't *want* to."

Please notice in the above statements the connotation of intent. People with ADHD have no particular desire to make others miserable, we simply want our needs met and the ability to contemplate the impact of our actions on others can only happen when we stop to think about our actions. But the crux problem of ADHD is an inability to pause, to wait, to delay a response to the internal or external environment. Nowhere in the development of ADHD do we enjoy making others feel bad. We simply have a desire and cannot evacuate the impulse until it is met.

I wish it were easier to make those concerned parents understand the plight of the ADHD child whose needs are not met. When this happens, he does not simply feel annoyed or upset. For example, being denied a new toy he yearns for makes him feel as though an immediate, vast emptiness has opened inside him, a hunger that can never, ever be satiated. One that can be directly compared to the level of need experienced by the child whose physiological need (hunger, thirst, etc.) is left unfulfilled rather than a simple unsatisfied desire.

Once the child with ADHD is thwarted in his goal, a driving force beyond his volitional control is let loose. To say that the child feels helpless is mere euphemism, because that feeling of helplessness results from the child's inability to impact on the outside world.

As I progressed through grade school, my failures mounted up. Never once did anyone stop and wonder just why I was not managing to progress. In third grade, when we were learning the multiplication tables, Miss Vlass punished my failure to memorize them by writing the answer to seven times eight on a board and hanging it around my neck. I had to wear that sign for the rest of the day, while my classmates poked fun and jeered. Now, children with ADHD have major problems with short-term memory recall. Why? Not because they are not as bright as anybody else, but because their attention hops from one thing to another the way a butterfly goes from flower to flower. It just does not stay in place long enough to engrave multiplication tables on the memory – or at least, not without using special learning techniques which are rarely applied, even in the classrooms of today. Perhaps I have never forgotten the answer to seven times eight (I think it is fifty … something), but nor have I forgotten the humiliation and degradation of having been singled out in such a cruel way. And I am not alone. My experience is mirrored by that of hundreds of thousands, even millions, of contemporary Americans, many of whom are living through it right now. Is the situation better? Well, for those ADHD children who are identified and treated appropriately, it is. But it is not as much better as it should be. We know a thousand times more about ADHD than we used to, but those lessons are usually not properly applied to the ADHD child struggling with school. For example, Jonathan is a bright boy with a healthy, average intellectual endowment. But because he has a difficult time with math (due to his ADHD, not his ability to learn per se) he has been placed in a below average math class and has even been recommended to *repeat* that math class next year. Not once has his school suggested that they provide remedial help for him. It is caught in the box of dogmatic old world thinking and openly refuses to think beyond the box and fix the problem. Fortunately, Jonathan's parents are not going to let the school lower the bar of academic excellence for their son and they are going to get him the help he needs at their own expense. The school did not for one second consider the impact their recommendation will have on the child but simply opted for what would be easiest, and cheapest, for them!

Every day spent in my office brings me new stories of injustice done to children with ADHD by their teachers. An eleven year old boy named Jonathan, the same boy mentioned above, recently told me of a problem he experienced:

"I was throwing a wad of tape back and forth with a friend of mine while the teacher was out in the hall. This other kid got in our way, so I hit him in the head with the ball of tape. He threw the tape back at me and when he missed, I told him he threw like a girl. I started to go back to my seat and all of a sudden he tackled me from behind and we both fell into the desks and made a loud noise. The teacher came and told the other kid to go to the seat, and sent me to the Principal's office. I know I started it, but he was the one who tackled me and I was the one who got in trouble. I know I should not have thrown the tape ball in the first place, but he was the one who tackled me. Shouldn't he have got in more trouble? All I did was throw tape while he tackled me and knocked over desks."

Jonathan was suspended for three days for fighting, although this was the first time he had ever been found to have a problem with aggression, while his adversary was given detention for half an hour. Admittedly, Jonathan has ADHD and this was not the first time he had a disciplinary problem. Nonetheless, the teacher acted harshly and quickly without giving any leeway at all for the impact of ADHD on Jonathan's behavior. Sure, Jonathan deserved to be punished for throwing things in the classroom. But he also needed to be praised for not overreacting to the attack and allowing the fight to escalate to epic proportions. Above all, he did not deserve to be treated differently than one of his classmates simply because he suffers from a disability.

When I was in fifth grade, Miss Mascari made me stand at the head of the room and face the class because I was not behaving consistently with her model of appropriate classroom etiquette. I wanted to talk to one of my friends in the row behind, and turned to face him while she instructed us on one topic or another. Instead of trying to reason with me, or offering an incentive to sit still, she chose to make me feel stupid, and undeserving of being part of the class: "If you are not prepared to behave yourself, then I am not obliged to treat you as a member of this class. You can stand at the head of the class until you are ready to apologize and start to behave like a civilized human being."

Teachers should never underestimate the impact of humiliation on a child's psyche. I am a middle-aged man, and I still remember as if they had happened yesterday the many episodes when I was singled out for especially harsh punishment. As a successful professional, I am one of the few fortunate ADHD sufferers who "got away". Too many of my peers reached maturity without *ever* having encountered a sympathetic teacher, and without realizing that they could succeed at work or at college. They still suffer from educational inadequacies as a result. Our prisons, and the ranks of the homeless are swollen by individuals with undiagnosed or untreated ADHD. How many of these people's lives would not have been wasted if they had been helped to make the most of the educational resources available to them? How much of the taxpayer's money could be spent on schools and libraries and sports facilities instead of prisons, social welfare and drug rehabilitation? Providing the ADHD child with the help he needs – *while he is still a child* – costs little in terms of dollars and cents, and relatively little in terms of time invested, but it can truly make all the difference in the life of an individual. The society that cares for its more vulnerable members and helps them to grow is a civilized one.

When it comes to setting standards for appropriate behavior in the classroom and elsewhere, adults should lead the way in showing children that it is not acceptable to single out one of their peers and make his life a misery on the grounds of real or perceived difference. I think that I was in third grade when my classmates became increasingly aware that I was not the same as them, and the teasing, name-calling and bullying became more intense. As kindergarten recedes into the distance, children become increasingly aware of themselves as social beings, and ever less tolerant of the habitual outsider. Viewing kids through the soft-focus lens of sentimentality is a fool's game. As anyone who has spent time with children knows, they can be as merciless as a pack of wolves and turn on the weakest among them with the greatest of ease, positively relishing in his or her pathetic cries and whimpers. And I am not talking about exceptionally brutal childhood bullies. Alas, this behavior is typical of the worst aspect of the group behavior of generally well-adjusted children, from ordinary, loving families. The teachers in my school must have known what was going on, but because they had already categorized me as a difficult, wayward child, they were not inclined to be sympathetic. I told on the other children for a while, but with responses like, "Don't be a tattle-tale!" "What are you doing to provoke them?" "If you behave the way you usually do, I am not surprised," and "Why don't you just stand up for yourself?" (arguments that cannot help but remind one of the sort of treatment rape victims sometimes get in court), I soon learned to withdraw into myself and deal with the bullying as best I could – usually by running away and hiding.

I might have been unpopular and unacademic but I certainly was not so stupid that I was willing to get beaten up, even if the teachers seemed to think that I did not matter very much. I did not want to get hurt, but the jeers and insults still wounded, and I spent too many nights brooding and crying in my room. No matter how long and hard I pondered the problem, I just could not figure out what I was doing to make myself so deeply despised. I stared at myself in the mirror on the bedroom wall, trying to see if I looked different in any way. Was I particularly ugly, so much so that the other kids could not bear to look at me? Apparently not. Had someone been spreading lies about me? Were the teachers involved in some sort of a co... telling the children to be mean to me behind my back? Did God hate me so much that even *he* had abandoned me? I never stopped asking myself questions, but no matter how long and hard I thought, I just could not come up with any satisfactory answers.

Adults should never underestimate children's potential for cruelty to their peers; the school yard and bus can be the most hostile environments that any child encounters and those pint-size adversaries who may look so cute are real, terrifying tormentors to their victims. For many people, being bullied at school is the most frightening and traumatic experience they encounter, ever. Being different makes it all the worse, whether the child in question is a member of an ethnic minority, physically atypical in some way, or has a developmental disability such as ADHD. In my case, my classmates chose a particularly vicious nickname for me (I will not even repeat it here) and gleefully used it on every possible occasion.

When I was still in grade school, I developed a passionate crush on a little girl named Maria. I thought that she was the most beautiful thing I had ever seen, and I worshipped her from a distance, watching the swoop of her dark hair as she bent over to erase an error on a page, and the way she straightened her skirt when she rose from her desk to answer a question on the blackboard. I already "knew" that I was a lowly creature, and that there was little point in trying to approach her. I did not resent this fact, and was happy to look on in silent admiration. Then, one day, we both rose from our seats on the school bus at the same time, and I saw an opportunity to show Maria that I could be a gentleman, despite everything. "Please," I told her. "After you." Maria looked straight at me, with contempt written all over her pretty face, and uttered just one word – *that* nickname. She was no better than any of the other children in the class, and I was utterly destroyed. Maria probably never gave it a second thought, but I cried for days.

Both of us had internalized the idea that I was a *bad person*. Not that I was a person who sometimes did bad things, or a person who had difficulty concentrating in class but a bad person. She obviously thought that as such, I deserved whatever ugly name the other children chose to give me, and you know what? I did too. Maria's rejection of my attempt to be polite broke my heart and left me even more angry, distraught and isolated than before.

I wish that I could tell you that things have changed in the school yards and buses of modern America. They have not. The child who is "different" is still singled out for cruel, abusive treatment at the hands of his peers. Never forget that not all bullies are exceptionally troubled, vicious children from tough neighborhoods and "bad" families. Ordinary, well-brought up kids can be unspeakably vicious when they group together and a "pack mentality" develops. We should never make the mistake of sentimentalizing children or childhood. Children have been described by anthropologists as "the original savage tribe", and that assessment is really not so far from the truth! Meanwhile, far too many teachers look on complacently, even with complicity, as their own prejudiced opinion about children with ADHD makes them think that they are actually "getting what they deserve".

School, then, was a minefield of potential calamities for me. And it seemed that I could never fully escape from its restrictions, even when I was in the family home. My bedroom represented a degree of security, but home was far from being the refuge it should have been. Mom and Dad were worried about my apparent lack of academic ability and although they did not know how to help, they did try. They were sure that all I needed to do was concentrate and stop fooling around, and then everything would start to be alright. And they tried to help me to accomplish these goals by punishing me when I failed to meet them. Homework was a constant source of tension in our house.

"Dick," Dad would say. "You just go straight up to your room and don't come out until you've done your homework properly."

"But, Dad …" I would protest. "I've already done my homework. I *can't* do it any better."

"Listen to your father!" Mom would interject. "If he says it's not done right, it isn't. Now get upstairs!" And off I would go, dragging my heels along the carpet and feeling dejected.

"There's no point," I would mutter. "I can't do it any better. I already tried."

Despite my indignation, I did not really mind going to my room. It was the only place where I felt completely safe, and although I could not do my homework properly, I did have some fun playing with my things and looking through my private possessions. I still have the desk I used as a boy for doing my homework – the inside drawer is covered in childish graffiti testifying to a thousand lonely evenings upstairs in my room. But I just could not understand the point of struggling and laboring over a task I *knew* I could not complete anyway and, most evenings, I did not even try. By the time I was supposed to be old enough to tackle an hour or more of homework, I had been taught to have no faith in my abilities. I was sure that I would never be able to do the work I was supposed to be learning at school.

Dad never helped me to master the challenge of doing my homework, but I cannot really blame him in any way for not assisting me. He was just saying what every parent said in those days: "Go and do your homework." He expected me to understand and be able to live up to the standards that he had set for me. There was little understanding of the fact that some children need more help than others and no tolerance of the child who was different in any significant way.

As a psychologist, I encounter ADHD kids who are going through the same torment that I did as a little boy. As an exercise to illustrate how attitude affects academic performance, I often give them an impossible puzzle to try to solve. It goes like this: At the top of a page, I write the words "gas" "electric" and "water". At the bottom of the page, I draw three icons representing houses. Then, I give the following instructions: "Each of these new houses needs to be connected to each utility. Your job is to draw a line from each utility to each house. You need to draw a line from every house to every utility, but no line can cross another, or go behind a utility."

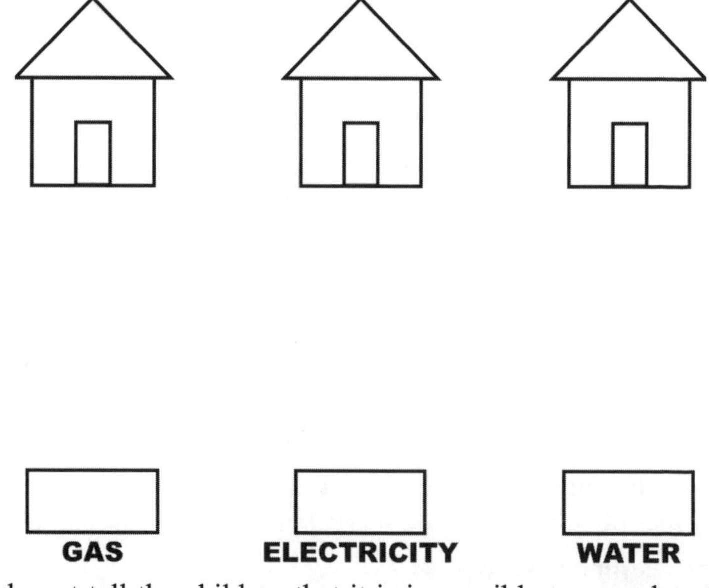

I do not tell the children that it is impossible to complete the task, which is in fact the case. Because they believe that there is a solution and that they have the ability to solve the puzzle, the kids always put in a solid effort. The lesson to be learned here is that, when children believe that they have the ability to do something, they really try. But once they are told that the task is impossible, the effort stops. Likewise, when children believe, correctly or otherwise, that they cannot accomplish a task such as their homework, they do not put in any effort.

Instead, when they believe in themselves and their ability to be successful, effort follows. Unfortunately, most ADHD kids are rarely given the opportunity to believe in their own capacity to succeed.

7
Why does my teacher hate me?

I hear what you are saying, but with thirty kids in my class, I just don't have time to make any exceptions, and that includes ADHD… grade school teacher.

Today, we know that many children have ADHD, but many of them still do not receive the help they need to succeed in school, and wind up with educational, psychological and emotional deficiencies that will haunt them for the rest of their lives.

I meet ADHD kids representing every stage of the intellectual spectrum in my office. Few are allowed to reach their potential and many parents, like mine, while loving their child and wanting the very best for him, become agents in his downfall. Not because of any lack of affection or good intentions, but because they have never been taught about realistic ways to deal with ADHD and are forced to resort in the traditional methods of punishment and chastisement.

Although many children who have ADHD also have learning disabilities, it is a mistake to assume that they are less intellectually gifted than children without the condition. In fact, many ADHD children have high levels of intelligence and creativity and, with the right help, can proceed to be successful at college and in their subsequent careers. Many of the kids I meet in my office are bright, charming and talented. They also have ADHD. Whether or not they manage to grow into happy, successful adults depends in large part on the amount of help they are given in school. When I have to hear a child say, "My teacher hates me," and know that they might not be far from the truth, my heart sinks, because every day I see how far we have still to travel.

The challenge that faces parents and teachers is that of creating an environment in which ADHD children are able to develop their talents and use them constructively, while not causing any negative impact on the other students in the class. Unfortunately, many teachers give up without even trying, saying, "I have too many students to focus on just one," "I can't have one rule for some children and another rule for others," or "I have tried everything, he just *won't* (notice the reference to intent) respond."

Would a doctor be allowed to justify not treating a patient by saying that he does not respond well to antibiotics? I do not think so. Refusing to make allowances for the ADHD child in the classroom environment is downright unprofessional.

There are those who suggest that ADHD children should be educated separately, but this is not a viable long-term solution. Short-term or supplemental teaching designed for pupils with ADHD may be helpful in some cases, but people with ADHD are not going to grow up to live in isolation from the rest of society and they need to learn how to manage their condition in a broader context. One of the important functions of a school should be to help *all* of its students to grow up to become functional members of the society in which they will live, and this includes those students who are not always the easiest to deal with. Imagine the justifiable outrage there would be if a child who was an amputee was refused assistance in getting to the classroom to attend lessons, or a deaf child was not provided with a hearing apparatus! We should expect to see special help being given to pupils with ADHD, too. If discrimination is wrong, it is wrong. Period.

Many teachers do not believe that ADHD exists, and refuse to acknowledge it or make any adaptation in their teaching practice to accommodate the ADHD child. They say that children are being lazy, that parents are trying to excuse their childrearing deficiencies and that psychologists are only interested because they want to make a quick buck. Others take it upon themselves to make a diagnosis and demand that children be medicated, without making any commitment to participating in the behavior modification techniques that must accompany medication if a treatment plan is to have successful long-term consequences.[4]

So, we know that our education system is deficient in helping children with ADHD to overcome their disability, but how can we put it right? Will it require huge investments of time and money? Will the whole education system have to be overhauled? Well, no. In fact, most procedures which have a profoundly positive effect on kids with ADHD are inexpensive, simple and will work for the entire class.

Given the prevalence of ADHD, basic training in recognizing the disorder and implementing instructional techniques designed to help to deal with it should be provided. Currently, schools *are* legally obliged to accommodate the needs of students with ADHD, but many fall far short of doing so. In order for children to learn, the classroom must be an orderly environment, and pupils must be able to listen and respond to their teacher's instructions. All of this becomes much more difficult when there is an unassisted child with ADHD to deal with. Without meaning to disobey, he is likely to wander about the room, interrupt other children, and fail to listen to the lesson. When he is reprimanded, he will look at the teacher with wide-eyed bafflement, saying "But I was just …" "I only wanted …" "I had to tell something to …"

[4] Besides, if we medicate each and every child who presents with ADHD-like symptoms without verifying the diagnosis, we risk failing to identify kids whose behavior may be due to emotional trauma and abuse and who need different treatment, and possibly removal from a damaging situation, in order to become well.

It goes without saying that a teacher cannot be expected to work under these conditions – but this is *not* justification for lashing out at the child with ADHD. An adult should never set himself up as a child's adversary. "Pick on someone your own size," is what we tell bullies, and the same applies when those bullies are educators.

Striking a balance between being fair to the needs of the ADHD child and those of the other students can be a difficult chore to accomplish without some basic understanding of the condition, and techniques to help combat its symptoms. While the teacher needs to understand that the ADHD child's difficulties with sitting still, listening and obeying are not intentional, it is also true that he cannot be allowed to simply behave in any way he chooses, creating chaos in the classroom and preventing him and other children from learning. Having ADHD makes it harder to conform – but it is not a valid excuse for every act of defiance. Remember, ADHD is an explanation for why disruptive behavior occurs, but it is not an excuse for it! How to deal with the problems that inevitably arise? By behaving harshly and, worst of all, resorting to violence or humiliation, the problem will not be helped; it will only be made worse.

Remember that children learn even more from example than they do from instruction. If the adults around them use bullying, intimidation and verbal or physical violence, their young wards will soon start to do the same. My own experience of school quickly taught me that teachers were the enemy. They did not like me, and they made their feelings abundantly clear. How was I supposed to respect and obey them in these circumstances? It was impossible to please them, it seemed, so there was really no point in trying. They made it clear that they felt that I was stupid, bad and incorrigible and my failures were duly punished. I was given no help in improving and no incentive to wish to do so. My actions were treated as if they were volitional and the result of thought, not as impulsive and thoughtless. The biggest betrayal I felt resulted from the fact that their feelings about me were communicated directly to Mom and Dad, without any suggestions as to how I might be helped to achieve more:

"I'm afraid that Richard is a problem, Mrs. Kuendig. He just *won't* sit still. He *doesn't want* to listen. He *enjoys* tormenting the other children. You are just going to have to speak with him about his behavior. We can't have him here unless he improves."

Common disciplinary techniques used to keep all students in line, not just those with ADHD, include detention and suspension. Let's look at these practices for a moment. A child with ADHD has immense difficulty with learning and the classroom environment. He finds it hard to sit still while his limbs are taut with excitement, ready to bound into action. How can he listen to the teacher and complete homework assignments when he cannot concentrate on anything for more than five minutes? Almost invariably, he *hates* school, because it has come to represent frustration, failure and humiliation. Does detention make it easier in any way to follow the rules and to make academic progress? Absolutely not. It fosters resentment, self-hatred and anger. Do the inevitable suspensions teach him a lesson and make him vow to work harder in future? Hell, no! The child who hates school and habitually clashes with teachers and other authority figures is glad when he gets suspended. He is *delighted.* Enforced time away from the dreaded classroom? Why, that is exactly what he wanted! And what lesson has the child learned? Why, that if he behaves just as badly as he possibly can, he will be rewarded by being given two or three days off school!

When I was a school boy, there was nothing I liked better than being suspended. A day of suspension was an unscheduled day off, and the scolding I received from my parents did little to diminish my pleasure. "Hooray," I thought. "A whole day away from the stupid classroom. Even if Mom yells at me for an hour, that still leaves the rest of the day for having fun." It was a pretty elementary cost-benefit analysis.

I understand that the impact of suspension is designed to make the child's grades drop and thereby force them to want to avoid being suspended. But the ADHD child is different in three ways that need to be considered. First, the ADHD student is oriented to the here and now, eliminating present concern about future grades. Second, being out of school is experienced as a great reward, and the child is happier to be out of school that to be there. Third, they have already been taught to expect failure and low grades are taken as a given.

Many ADHD children are also made to repeat grades, as was I. At a cost to the State of thousands of dollars per child, this practice is counterproductive, making the child dislike school more than ever, boring him and forcing him to engage in the humiliation of having to interact with younger children. Perhaps worst of all, children who have repeated one grade are more likely than other kids to have to repeat yet another year! When a child "has" to repeat a grade, the fault is the teachers', and not his. There is also a strong correlation between grade retention and drug abuse. All the research shows that repeating grades is expensive, and counter-productive. So, why do children keep having to repeat when this clearly creates more problems than it solves? The answer is that it is easier for teachers to make a child repeat than admit to themselves and others that they have not provided him with quality instruction, designed to accommodate the ADHD disability, and attention.

There is plenty wrong with the way ADHD children are treated in American schools today, but putting it all right is feasible and the biggest investment required is an all-important investment in tolerance. To make the most of the school's environment, the ADHD child has to be able to count on the cooperation of parents and teachers, and techniques which can make all the difference can be surprisingly simple and easy to put in place. Teachers may feel, initially, that providing special help for ADHD children is extra work, but the bottom line is that a child who is no longer frustrated and unsuccessful will be much easier in the classroom. A little investment of time early in a child's school career has untold dividends as he grows and matures, and if their teacher says that they are too busy with the other thirty-five students in the class, well, it is time that they sought another career. Period.

Children with ADHD are not ignorant of being "different" from the other students in their class, and can be vulnerable to being bullied or, conversely, to becoming bullies themselves. Both situations must be dealt with quickly to avoid escalation. Both bullies and the bullied need help – the child who behaves aggressively towards his peers may be acting out feelings of fear, frustration and neediness, regardless of the unpleasantness of his behavior. Children (and adults, for that matter) are not always adept at expressing their feelings, and sensations of vulnerability can be expressed as aggression, especially when children are unable for one reason or another to express themselves verbally. Little boys may tend to resort more frequently to violence, while little girls may use the equally damaging forms of ostracization and verbal abuse. I have met boys who lashed out at teachers and peers after literally years of being belittled and humiliated in front of their classmates. They generally say that they " … didn't mean to" do it. One thing is for sure. It would have been a lot easier for them to control their runaway emotions if these had been recognized and cared for from the start.

Whatever the situation, however, bullying must not be tolerated. For me, elementary school represented torture. The other children despised me, and made their feelings clear. Worst of all, their behavior was tolerated and even accepted by the teaching staff, who were frustrated by me, and clearly felt that I deserved whatever I got. I was a nuisance. I made their jobs harder to do, and they resented me for it, instead of trying to help me learn techniques to behave better and intervening to stop the bullying. As I approached school every morning, my anxiety levels and tension grew until my stomach was in knots. Perhaps Mom and Dad were concerned, but publicly they towed the party line and told me to "stop complaining and stand up for myself." As I mentioned before, our society expects little boys to be able to behave like "men" long before they should even *aspire* to adult notions of heroism and bravery. We need to learn to allow our boy children to be just what they are – children.

Because ADHD compromises the individual's ability to maintain and persist in effort, homework represents an enormous challenge to the affected child who sees the hours stretch out before him in a seemingly endless series of torments and frustrations. The challenge that homework represents to the child with ADHD acquires mammoth proportions as they come home from school and start to dread the moment when Mom or Dad says that it is time to take out their books. By the time the evening meal has been completed and that awful moment is reached, the child's levels of tension have grown to the point whereby their already compromised attention span is damaged even further and, in stress and rage, they are ready to lash out at their parents in anger at their own inability to cope.

Parents of a child with ADHD have an extra responsibility in ensuring that he or she can deal with the daily chores that need to be completed. Children often react by having a tantrum when faced with duties that they do not want to fulfill, or that they feel unable to tackle. Because ADHD children tend to be immature for their age, these tantrums often continue for much longer than in the case of other children. Too often, the parents' response acts further to delay the completion of the homework. The result? The tantrum has succeeded in achieving the desired delay, and the child's behavior is reinforced. "Right," he thinks. "If I don't want to do my homework right after supper, all I have to do is kick up a fuss until we're all too tired to deal with it. That's easy. I can manage that!" Unless the pattern is interrupted, it is going to be like this every night, and who wants to spend their evenings having to deal with a screaming child?

Parents can make things easier by dividing the homework period into a series of easy-to-manage time slots, with regular breaks and little rewards when the child has accomplished what he is supposed to do, and teachers can help by adapting homework to the capabilities of the child. Of course, ADHD children need to demonstrate that they have grasped the message of a lesson, but they may be able to do this without completing the same bulk of work as the other children. If most of the kids in a class are told to do ten math exercises, perhaps the ADHD child can demonstrate proficiency by doing six in the same period of time.

Children with ADHD should not be exempt from doing homework, and they need to learn the same lessons as the other children in the class. However, completing a task typically takes them much longer than it does the normal child. Faced with an assignment that they know will take hours, the child can quickly become frustrated, angry and defiant: "I can't do it. You can't make me do it. It's stupid. It's boring. I want to stop doing it *right now*. That's it, I'm out of here."

As you know, one of the primary symptoms of ADHD is the difficulty of maintaining effort over time. When a child knows that he is going to have to be able to concentrate for a whole hour, the task can just seem too daunting and instead of making an effort, he will rebel and resist, making himself so angry in the process that concentration becomes even more difficult than it already is. Two or three periods of concentration of ten or fifteen minutes each might be manageable, however. Teachers can help, not by giving the child a different assignment, but by reducing its length. The amount of time he spends doing the work will be the same, and the reduced number of tasks will fill the same function of revealing whether or not he has understood and mastered the challenge. Never forget that fairness is not about giving everyone the same thing, but about giving everybody what they need.

Before instigating any techniques to help with difficult behavior, teachers should try to establish rapport with each of the children in their class, spending the first few weeks of every school year getting to know their students, and making sure that they understand what makes each child tick. This will make unruly behavior, if it arises, easier to deal with fairly and promptly and will help the child to see the teacher as a person rather than a fearful figure of authority. Similarly, it will help the teacher to recognize the humanity and the personality of the ADHD child, and to see his strengths as well as his weaknesses, making it possible to view him as a person with a need for special help, instead of just a problem in the classroom, an irritant that must be swept away. Throughout the year, a personal relationship between the teacher and the student can be maintained if the teacher ensures that he or she speaks to the child on an individual, personal level and not like an object, a piece of furniture that is broken and needs to be thrown out.

It does not take a degree in psychology to understand that when an individual is repeatedly told, either verbally or otherwise, that he is stupid, he will come to believe this. I certainly did. It took me years to undo the lesson and even now, sensations of my own worthlessness still come back to haunt me. Because ADHD people invariably present with behavioral problems from an early age, they are particularly vulnerable to being told that they cannot do things because they are just "dumb". As a little boy, I had already absorbed this misinformation even before attending school, and the rough and tumble of the classroom and school yard also enforced this view.

If this pattern of enforcement of a belief of one's own stupidity is not eliminated as soon as it appears, the ADHD child grows up with a strong belief in his inherent inability to get things done. This creates massive difficulties with motivation: "If I am dumb *anyway*, why beat myself up over getting an assignment in on time?" "I already knew I was going to flunk – I might as well have fun in the process." When I was a boy, I spent as much time as possible in the woods instead of at school, or fooling around with my friends instead of listening to the teacher. When my patients tell me that their teachers dislike them and do not want to help them in any way, I am sometimes left almost without words, because I know that what they are telling me is probably correct.

Teaching a child that he is stupid is unforgivable. I already knew that I had problems mastering some skills that seemed to come easily to my friends and this was a constant source of frustration and pain, even if I was not able to explain my feelings clearly. Instead of helping me to overcome the extra difficulty I faced, my parents and teachers naively let me believe that I was struggling because of an inherent flaw or lack. That it was all my fault.

Beliefs formed in early childhood are the hardest to unlearn – from the age of just three or four, most children already have fixed ideas about the world and their place in it. I was fortunate in being able to "unlearn" the lesson much later in life, but many are not.

Self-fulfilling prophecies of failure can be particularly hard to deal with in families where ADHD is present in a parent as well as in the child, as was the case in the Kuendig home. The Mom or Dad in question may reinforce the child's feelings about the inevitability of failure by saying, "You're just like me. I was never able to sit still and work either," or "I guess we're just not a very smart family." This is wrong. While the parent will never have the chance to repeat grade school again, he or she can help to stop the cycle of abjection and failure from occurring all over again. We cannot live through our children or for them, but the satisfaction of seeing one's offspring learn how to clear hurdles that caused earlier generations to stumble and fall is without price. My Dad was of a generation that never understood the nature of ADHD, and he was left to struggle along with no support or understanding of what he had to deal with every day. The result? A man who, although bright and motivated, constantly had to change jobs and was unable to see that at least one of his offspring was struggling and needed help. Far from insisting that the school help me with my educational problems, Dad felt strongly that all I needed to do was work, and I would be just fine.

Our educational system is failing a large proportion of students, especially those with developmental disorders such as ADHD. There is a very simple reason for this failure: apathy. It is a constant source of dismay to me that things have changed so little since I was a child at school. If I had a dollar for every time I have heard a teacher tell me that they can do nothing to help their ADHD students because "the class is too big", I would be a wealthy man! Teaching is difficult, I accept that. And I am more than willing to recognize that teachers are truly among the most important members of our society, with the responsibility they hold for educating and forming the minds of the adults of the future. But they must never forget how much more difficult life is for the little boy or girl who has to deal not only with the already daunting challenges of a normal childhood, but also with the disability of ADHD. And they have ADHD *all the time*. It does not magically stop at weekends, or after school, or during summer vacation or because they really, really try to make it go away or because once or twice they managed to sit still and do their work all day long.

Children are not all the same, and no amount of yelling and coercion will make the unusual child conform. Quite the reverse. Parents, teachers, and government alike collude in making things much more difficult for people with ADHD than they should be. Invariably, teachers say that they want to help, and earnestly ask for advice, but when they are given even the simplest of suggestions as to how they can help to make the classroom a more amenable environment for the ADHD child, they do not have time and their acceptance that ADHD exists and that it is a real disability rapidly begins to wane. Recently, after giving a seminar to a group of parents and teachers, a teacher stopped and told me on her way out, that she was "not going to do all that stuff you talked about, these kids will just have to learn to survive like the rest of us." In a perfect world, I suppose that none of us would ever have to exert ourselves unduly to fulfill our professional duties. But guess what? Responsible jobs always incur having to work extra hard at times, having to go the extra mile. The dividends make it more than worth our while and can literally rewrite the future for the challenged child. Teachers must acknowledge that they have a responsibility to *all* of their pupils, not just those who find learning easy and discipline no burden.

Generally, my first contact with an ADHD child's teacher is positive. He or she assures me that they will do everything they can to help. Gradually, however, conditions are introduced until it is very clear what they are prepared to do. Nothing, or at least very little.

No-one would suggest that teaching an ADHD child is easy all the time – it certainly is not, and (as a man who was a horribly difficult student throughout much of my childhood) I can empathize with the teacher who has felt at times like screaming, tearing out his or her own hair or even imagining the bliss that would reign if the troublesome child could somehow be removed. However, providing special assistance and support is easier than not doing so. A child who is coping with the demands of school and homework and can see the results of his efforts for himself will be much less disruptive, angry and hard to manage than the child who is constantly frustrated by failure and by teachers' and classmates' inability to understand him. The child whose disability is managed and compensated for is a better student than the child who is disabled, and is left to fend for himself. Unfortunately, however, there are many examples of the opposite occurring, as in the case of the ten year old whose spelling is great but who, because of his problems with fine motor control, opts to print rather than write in cursive. The teacher who seeks absolute compliance rather than correct spelling deducts five points from the spelling test because of the "wrong" handwriting. It seems incredible, doesn't it? After all, it was supposed to be a spelling test, not a handwriting test! But as my patient Skippy has now learned, it does not matter to the teacher whether or not he knows how to spell. Even if he gets all the words right, the teacher will still deduct points – as if this little boy with ADHD did not have enough to worry about already. Now, those five points might not seem like such a big deal to an adult, or to a child without ADHD, but in Skippy's case, the lesson he has learned is that his efforts are not appreciated. He has not been rewarded for his achievements, but punished for a "deficit" which should not have been relevant in the case of a spelling test. No effort was made to use a disability perspective. The teacher's behavior was at best discouraging and, at worst, illegal. After speaking with Skippy in my office, I found him to be heartbroken and bereft. "I spelled them *all* right," he said through his sobs. "But I still didn't get 100. I never get anything right." At our last session together on October 21st, 2002, Skippy asked, "Why should I bother studying so hard, when I never get 100 anyway?" It was hard to know how to answer.

Skippy's is not an isolated case. A seven year old patient of mine was chastised for coloring a picture of a turkey with unconventional colors and for coloring outside the lines. "You can do better than this," was the teacher's remark (I wonder what she thinks of the Expressionist movement in art …). She went on to say, "You've done better before, so I know that you are just being lazy now. I know that you can do better." People with ADHD are chastised almost as often for doing a *good* job as they are for doing a bad one! As Dr. Russell Barkley remarked to me once, "People with ADHD do well once and are punished for it for the rest of their lives." Teachers who meet the ADHD child on the one day in the year when he excels in some area use this as the basis of the belief that the ADHD is not really holding them back. They've proven that they can do things right, and failing to do so is clearly willful and deliberate. This assumption is absolutely untrue. Variability of behavior is a hallmark of ADHD, and when teachers tell a child that they can do something or other because they have done it before, the child begins to assume that the teacher is correct, and to become increasingly self-questioning and doubtful about themselves.

So, what should a teacher do? First of all, it is important to remember that punishment – such as deducting five points from a correct spelling test for flaws in handwriting – will never encourage the child to follow rules and will instead reinforce the notion in the child that his efforts are unnoticed and that he can never do anything right, no matter how hard he tries.

In psychology, use is made of a concept known as "shaping". This refers to the use of rewards when approximations of the desired end result behavior are achieved. In other words, if you want a child to write in cursive script, you start by rewarding minor attempts to accomplish this, and then progressively larger attempts until at last the child has become able to master an entire task. Essentially, in order to get a child to comply with a certain behavioral directive in the classroom, the task in question is broken into its component parts, and successful completion of each component is rewarded until the complete desired behavior has been conquered.

"Success breeds success and failure breeds failure," is a saying I use often. If you want your child or student to succeed you must start by *creating* that success. Just as prophecies of failure are often self-fulfilling to a large extent, so can prophecies of success be! “It will be hard at first, but I know that I can do it eventually, and that my teacher will praise me,” is a much better lesson for the child to learn than the assumption that he is stupid and will “never be able” to master the new task. I never cease to be amazed to find teachers who have the opportunity to reward appropriate behavior in school but do not do so. There is a general tendency to suppose that the child must do something special to receive praise. The ADHD child, by sitting quietly and doing his work in an orderly fashion, *is* doing something special, and an opportunity to reward his good behavior has presented itself. By noticing and praising the child, the teacher has made it clear that he can be good, and that efforts to continue will be rewarded. Motivation for continuing to be good, and for striving to be better, has been established: “I sat quietly all day, and my teacher said that I was a good boy. If I do all my work neatly tomorrow, maybe she’ll let me use the computer by myself!” By ignoring the student when he conforms to desired behaviors, he will learn that there is “no point” in trying to accede to the teacher’s demands, which probably run contrary to the neurophysiology of the child with ADHD.

The idea that “normal” behavior should be rewarded is one that is foreign to many people. But if responsible adults let children with ADHD – or indeed *any* child – miss the chance to be encouraged, rewarded and praised, the opportunity to provide an example of human compassion has been missed, along with a chance to reinforce positive behavior. Teachers and parents alike need to decide how many rewards each work period will yield before the period even begins and then see to it that each child who behaves appropriately receives the reward he deserves. These rewards may take the form of symbolic tokens which can be accumulated over time until the child can “cash them in” for a larger reward. Far from it being the child’s responsibility to earn the tokens, it is the teacher's to make sure that the rewards are given every time the child is being good! Remember, shaping means that you reward small components of the desired end result behavior rather than waiting for the whole enchilada. Simply put, it is the adult's responsibility to find behavior to reward much more than it is the child's to emit some behavior that is demanded by the environment.

"But, Dr. Kuendig," the teachers protest when I suggest rewarding positive behavior. "I can't treat one of the kids differently to the rest. It just isn't fair."

Hello! Does it not seem like a lot of teachers really need to acquire a disability perspective here? I am not suggesting that they devote all of their time to one needy child, but simply that they acknowledge when he does the best he can. Being fair to all of the children in a class is not about treating them all the same way, it is about giving them all the help they need. Some kids do not need a lot of help, some need to sit near the front of the room because they do not hear so well, some need assistance to boost their confidence, and some find it hard to keep up because ADHD is preventing them from concentrating.

The vital key to improving the lot of ADHD kids in the school environment is knowledge. Considering the very high percentage of children who are diagnosed as having ADHD – not to mention the legions of undiagnosed cases – any teacher training program should include some basic information about the condition, what causes it, and how academic and social performance can be optimized. And the buck does not stop there. This understanding must be applied to the classroom. Let us look at some of the ways in which educators can work with children with ADHD to help them to overcome the extra challenges they face[5].

---

[4] The section that follows is strongly influenced by Russell Barkley, *ADHD in Children, Adolescents and Adults: Diagnosis, Assessment and Treatment.*

People with ADHD have serious problems managing time. In order to make large assignments practicable, teachers should divide them into short, manageable slots. They also have enormous difficulty managing their time and sustaining effort over time. The thought of having to stick to a particular activity for a prolonged period can be so overwhelming that ADHD students will be unable to complete the project. Instead of giving the class fifty questions to answer and an hour to complete the assignment, have them answer ten at a time, pausing for a moment after each batch of questions has been answered. This will give fidgety children the chance to move, shake aching arms and legs and turn their attention elsewhere before they have to return to the business at hand.

Crucial information that children must know is more likely to sink in if they are presented with a visual representation of it. It is worth having the classroom rules written out and posted clearly at the top of the classroom, with verbal reminders to students to read them through, or pasting a copy of the rules onto individual students' desks so that they will not forget what it is they have to do. When there are tests to be taken, teachers can write down the approach that students should take and display the instructions prominently.

There will be times when teachers have to chastise students, but there are *never* times when nagging and complaining endlessly yields effective results. Instead of subjecting the unruly child to a humiliating and boring lecture, teachers should take positive steps to help him to improve his behavior. When students spend the day sitting quietly and doing their work, do well in a test and conquer challenges, even a verbal acknowledgement will make them feel good and reinforce the desire to continue doing well, and receive still more.

Children with ADHD (and all children, to a lesser extent) are, among other things, problems waiting to happen! Instructors should never work under the false assumption that everything will go smoothly. Unless a plan of action is in place, teachers will find themselves psychologically and practically unprepared to deal with disruptive behavior and minor crises. If, instead, they have already mentally rehearsed what they intend to do in the event of having to cope with misbehavior in the classroom, they will be able to maintain the calm and authority they will need to bring the scene to a dignified end.

When a child is habitually disruptive, it is easy to fall into the trap of over-reacting to his every misdeed. Of course, dangerous or severely disruptive behavior must be interrupted, for everybody's sake, but flying off the handle when a minor classroom rule is broken will simply foster further defiance. If a student finds it hard to remember not to talk to his friends during class, the teacher may be able to come to an agreement with him whereby a gentle tap on the shoulder serves as a reminder that it is class-time, not time to chat. Serious misconduct warrants serious disciplinary action. Minor infringements of classroom by-laws do not.

If the errant student is never allowed to move on from his misdeeds, it will be extremely difficult for him to find the motivation he needs to improve. By all means, take the necessary steps to caution and discipline the child when he seriously misbehaves, but once the punishment or the reprimand has been given, move on. Start with a clean slate; everybody deserves a second chance.

There are times when the ADHD child does not respond well to behavioral management, when, even though a disability perspective is in place and help is available, he simply misbehaves. Should he be allowed to get away with this? Absolutely not. However, punishment should not give the child the impression that he is considered to be a bad person. It must always be clear that his behavior is bad, not him. Teachers should never use their position of authority to humiliate the child in front of his peers. Effective ways of dealing with out-of-control unruliness include removing the child from the situation to sit in a quiet place outside the classroom, confiscation of some of the tokens he has earned by being good on other occasions, and the like.

Teachers and ADHD students can work together to transform disruptive behavior into conformist behavior. Although ADHD is never a valid excuse for misbehaving, teachers can go a long way towards minimizing misbehavior and the consequent vicious cycle of punishment, resentment, and repeated misbehavior. Take, for example, the ADHD child's tendency to fidget, to leave his chair and to wander round the classroom. It goes without saying that this can be extremely disruptive and disturbing for the rest of the class. On the other hand, the urge to move on the part of the child is literally irresistible. How to reconcile these two facts? Teachers can make it legitimate for the child to leave his seat and walk around by making him responsible for carrying messages from one classroom to another, by asking him to erase writing from the blackboard, by allowing him to change position so long as it does not interfere with his work, and by praising him for staying still when he must. As non-ADHD children also benefit from being allowed to move from time to time, the whole class can occasionally be involved in brief periods of physical activity. Children whose motor control is weak can be helped by providing chalk holders and a degree of leniency about standards of neatness. Teachers can maintain contact with all members of the class by arranging the desks in such a manner that eye contact can be established with all students at all times. If a teacher's goals for the students are realistic, and can be adapted to the ADHD child, they will be met, if not all the time, then as much of the time as possible, removing or reducing the need for chastisement and significantly lightening the burden of stress that bears upon both teacher and ADHD child. Teachers must remember that, although the disability is not visible in physical terms, the ADHD individual is disabled. Bearing this in mind, rules may need to be repeated or visually represented, appropriate behavior rewarded rather than taken for granted, and flexibility put in place of inflexibility. Even quite simple tasks may need to be explained and demonstrated step-by-step, always bearing in mind that the students who need the most help are often also the students who are most loath to ask for it.

This may all sound like a lot of extra work, but it really is not. The skills that teachers acquire in learning how to maximize the potential of ADHD students will also be useful in educating the entire class. All kids have their ADHD moments! Furthermore, literally none of the interventions that can make all the difference in helping the ADHD child are costly (specialized equipment is not necessary; patience and tolerance are) while the rewards are priceless.

In generations past, blind children were thought to be without hope: "They will never be useful members of society". Many people assumed that they were also mentally deficient, and they were at risk of spending their lives in asylums (especially if they were also deaf and/or mute) or of being reduced to a miserable existence, living off the charity of their families, on the streets or in wretched workhouses. Fortunately, realizing that the blind have an extra hurdle to clear but are not less intelligent than the rest of us, educational expert Mr. Braille devised a system of reading and writing especially adapted to their needs. Today, we take it for granted that children who cannot see will be taught how to use Braille, and how to take advantage of all the technologies that enable them to be fully functional, independent adults. Similar adaptations have been made to accommodate the various needs of deaf children, children with physical disabilities of one kind or another, and people with readily identifiable and recognizable mental disabilities. And that is just how it should be. Why, then, do we not make similar arrangements for children with ADHD? Arguably, the hurdles that they have to clear should be less daunting than they are for many blind or otherwise physically disabled individuals. We know that, with treatment and help many, if not most, individuals with ADHD can be as successful professionally and personally as their non-ADHD peers. But still, those hurdles are *not* being jumped. Why? Because special provisions are not being made, and special tools are not being provided. Collectively, we should be ashamed. The plaintive cry of the child with ADHD, "Why does my teacher hate me?" should make us hang our heads in shame.

8
Growing up ADHD

"Remember when you had a party? All the salt spoons were stolen and used for drugs. And then there was the time that you and your friend stole Mother's purse and let everyone believe that someone had broken into the house. The police were called and everything ..."
– Libby Kuendig.

Me as a teen. If I had thought childhood was hard, some really unpleasant times lay ahead.

Remember that ADHD kids have a developmental disability, and that they tend to be immature for their age. In most people, adolescence is generally considered to end in the late teens – that is why we extend the right to vote to young people of eighteen, and often set the age of consent even lower than that. In the case of the person with ADHD, it is more realistic to consider the end of adolescence to occur in the mid twenties. When I diagnose a child as having ADHD, I tell parents to expect to have to support him or her, financially, emotionally and otherwise, until the age of 25 or so. In my case, adolescence effectively ended after my fiancée left me, when I decided to go to college at the age of 22. The years before then were probably even more difficult and distressing than those of my early childhood, both to me and to my parents.

When I reached puberty, the problems that had plagued me throughout my childhood did not go away. They got worse, much worse. School was a nightmare. I continued to get low grades, and clashes with teachers were constant. A majority – about 65% – of children with ADHD develop Oppositional Defiant Disorder (ODD) and I had a full-blown case. I was a disciplinary nightmare for both my parents and my teachers, and I could see no reason why I should make any effort to change. To tell the truth, I did not even think that this was possible. By that time, I had learned that I was truly bad. Not just a bad student, or bad at math, or a bad athlete. Bad, per se. A *Bad Person.* A throwaway child. A disposable human being. I believed I could not do anything right, no matter how hard I tried, so I did not care. I was already damned anyway, so why not just have fun? After all, those who have ADHD live for the moment, and as I had already absorbed the message that I was a problem child, I had nothing to worry about.

Fun was easy, and personal judgment not an issue. Together with a few of my friends, I started smoking pot and experimenting with other drugs when I was about twelve or thirteen. Now *that* was fun. What a blast! Getting high quickly became one of my favorite pastimes. The sensations the drugs gave me allowed me to forget who I really was and to simply relax, let loose and go wild. Although they did not find out about the drugs until later, my parents were concerned about me, and sent me off to see various mental health professionals, whom I held in the deepest of disdain (quite rightly, as it happens). I remember one handing me a pencil and then pompously writing down that I was right-handed when I held it with that hand while I looked on in outrage. I already knew I was right-handed, for goodness' sake! "I might be stupid," I thought. "But I am not *that* stupid." Others were just as inept. Poor Mom and Dad were really wasting their money.

Undoubtedly, my situation in adolescence would have been better if I had had the benefit of some positive treatment as a child. As bad as things are now, there was little or no understanding of ADHD (or hyperactivity, as it was then called) when I was growing up. I could swagger as well as the next teenaged boy and I was physically well-formed and healthy, but the fears that had plagued my childhood had not gone away, and I still spent many lonely hours in my room, crying because I just could not understand why the world seemed to be a different place to me than to everybody else. And now I was even more ashamed of my tears. Not only was I a boy, and boys were not supposed to cry, I was too old to show my feelings, too. "Get a grip," I would mutter to myself angrily. "Just stop. Grow up." My self-admonishment never worked.

I struggled to understand the way society worked, and failed: "Why don't they understand?" "Why don't they see things the way I do?" "Am I just doing everything wrong or is the world always a cruel place?" Again, there are times when patriarchy fails boys and men even more than it does girls and women. For a male or boy to admit to feelings of fear, nervousness and having to seek comfort is extremely difficult, let alone having to admit to tears, and there are few teenage boys who will confide these sensations in anyone. Quite rightly, they know that they will probably be laughed at, and told to grow up and be men: "What are you? A little girl? You should be ashamed of yourself!" I know how Dad would have reacted if I had gone to him in tears.

Life remained a roller-coaster ride as I was torn between my desire to experiment and have fun – *all the time* – and the feelings of inadequacy which were reinforced by most of my encounters with authority figures and my peers. My teachers largely seemed to agree with my self-assessment as a lost cause, and I had become unable to judge my classmates' reactions to me with any degree of objectivity. When they laughed, I was sure that they were making fun of me. When they invited me to join them at some activity or other, I suspected a cruel joke. When someone called, "Hey, Dick!" I tensed, waiting for the rebuke or jeer at my expense.

Like a large percentage of teens with ADHD and considerable numbers of normal teens, drugs held a huge attraction for me from the very first time I got high. Reality stunk, so why shouldn't I try to experience something else? There was hardly a drug I would not take, just for the hell of it. The mechanism that makes most people at least stop and think about whether they want to do something or not was simply lacking in me. I had no emotional brakes to slow me down – and plenty of normal teenagers find it hard to resist the allure of a psychedelic experience as it is. A new way of relating to the world? I was all for it! The idea that I might be risking my health, or making myself vulnerable to being arrested did not matter a damn to me. The phrase "seize the day" might have been written for me; delayed gratification was not in my vocabulary. ("Smoking can cause long-term health damage? But I'm just fifteen! I might be dead by the time I'm twenty-five. That's years away!" "Drug addiction? Nah, I'm getting high *today*. Tomorrow I'll probably be doing something else.") A drugs counselor came to our school to warn us that getting high could lead to falling grades. Did I care? I did not. My grades could not fall much lower, anyway.

One day, I was in English class in the throes of an Acid trip when the school psychologist knocked on the door and asked me to come out and have a word with him. There I stood in the hall, watching the students' lockers buckle and dance and listening as he told me that he felt that I was making progress. I was even in class when I was supposed to be. It was the funniest thing I had ever heard. There he was, praising me for my "improvement" while in reality, I was confirming to myself my expertise in manipulating the system. He was praising me for being responsible and sober while, at that very moment, I was nothing of the sort.

"You have *got* to be the stupidest person I've ever met," I thought. "You're standing in front of someone who's tripping his brains out, and you have just no idea." I couldn't stop myself from laughing as I watched the world spin. Perhaps he thought that it was youthful exuberance.

The 1960s was an exciting decade in America, and it was also a stressful one. The Vietnam war had started and it seemed like every second day a riot broke out somewhere. Rioting was contagious – it even spread to our school on the peaceful east coast. On the day of the disturbance, I was in Home Economics class, where I was supposed to be, for once in my life. I liked Home Economics. Free food? Of course! Anyway, I was sitting there waiting for the homemade pizza to finish cooking when I looked outside the window and saw all hell break loose on the school grounds. Interested as I was in being rebellious, I was even more interested in pizza. After all, I had been living a rebellion on my own for some time by then.

"Well, look at that," I thought to myself with little more than mild curiosity. "A riot." And I turned my attention to the oven timer. The smell of cooking dough and melting cheese was filling the air, and it was a lot more interesting than whatever was going on outside. I stayed put, savored my pizza with relish and went home without giving the riot a second thought. That evening, the phone rang. It was Principal Fallon, summoning my father and I to school the following morning for an urgent meeting.

"Dick is in big trouble," he said. "He has been caught instigating a riot. This goes beyond mischief. This is going to call for some serious intervention."

Dad groaned, and as soon as he hung up he started to yell, "You damn idiot! Are you trying to destroy this family? Are you trying to end up in jail? You are certainly heading in the right direction ..." He was working himself up for an all-out battle.

"Hold on a minute," I interrupted. "I wasn't there. I was in Home Economics eating pizza." I was full of righteous indignation. It is bad enough getting in trouble when you *have* done something, but when you have not done anything at all? No way! I was not about to let them pin this one on me. This time, I was not going to let myself get blamed for something I had not done, just because I had been at fault before. I was going to stand and fight my ground, but my history of ADHD behavior was haunting me and my reputation was everyone else's guiding philosophy.

Dad paused for breath.

"Can you prove it?" he asked, cautiously. He was not inclined to trust me, but he did not want to believe that I was a rebel-rouser, a rioter. That was in a whole different category of trouble-making. I managed to calm him down, and we let things wait until the following day.

The next morning, we went down to the school, and I got the Home Economics teacher to write a note saying that I was indeed in class when the riot broke out. Then my Dad and I went to the principal's office, where Mr. Fallon was accompanied by a whole cadre of policemen, both uniformed and in plain clothes. He had an air of self-satisfied solemnity. I guess he was already imagining the exclusive he would give the local press: "Instigator of high school riot apprehended!" He was probably already coining phrases for the interview with the reporter, and imagining the cover photograph of me being led away in handcuffs, while he looked on with grim determination …

"I'm taking this very, very seriously," he told us pompously. He had been hoping to find a way to make me leave since day one, and now I was to be arrested for having started a riot. Mr. Fallon could not have been happier. The papers for my arrest had already been drawn up, and in the accuser's eyes, I had already been tried and condemned, as is often the case with people who are on the high maintenance end of the behavioral spectrum. So far as he was concerned, there was no room in his school for a boy like me. I did not fit into his parameters for normal adolescence.

Dad knew that this time I was not to blame for anything. Sitting down, he asked for a copy of my schedule.

"Dick was supposed to be in Home Economics," the principal told us. "But he was seen – in fact, I saw him myself – out on the sports field inciting the other kids to riot. He is in big trouble this time, Mr. Kuendig. This time he has really gone too far. I can't say I was surprised to see him, either. Dick has been nothing but bad news since the first day he came into this school. Why, if you had been there, you would have been just horrified to see the violence that your son is capable of …"

"I don't think so," Dad interrupted, showing him the note from the Home Economics teacher. "Dickie was in class from the beginning to the end. He couldn't possibly have started the riot. You must have seen some other young man."

Mr. Fallon was livid as he read the note. He turned to stare at me, bug-eyed with fury, "Who wrote this? There's no way a teacher wrote this! You wrote this yourself." His face turned red and a vein throbbed in his mottled neck, but he was not alone with me, and was obliged to follow protocol while the policemen tried to hide their smiles and coughed back their laughter. Most of us enjoy the sight of an authority figure being cut down to size, and the cops were no exception.

The Home Economics teacher was duly summoned, and she confirmed that I had been in class, much to the headmaster's chagrin. I was saved from immediate arrest by the police, but now Mr. Fallon had yet another grudge to hold against me; I was responsible for his having been humiliated, and he was not about to forgive me. It was just a matter of time before he found a different stick to beat me with.

Kids who are habitually difficult to deal with, and find school hard to manage, grow used to injustices like this. They are blamed when they are guilty, and they are blamed when they are not. Sure, ADHD teens can be disruptive – often unbearably so – but they are not inherently evil and they should never be assumed guilty without proof. Under these circumstances, what incentive do they have to strive to do their best? The most they can hope for is that someone will growl, "I see you managed to stay out of trouble for once." Today, professionals and enlightened parents and teachers know that the most effective way to obtain the best possible performance from an ADHD child or teenager is to use positive reinforcement; to identify when they are being good and acknowledge the behavior with the same level of intensity they would use in chastising. Remember that behavior management is like algebra. What is done to one side of the equation must be done to the other. For every misbehavior that is pointed out to a person with ADHD, at least two positive behaviors should be noted and praised. Unfortunately, many educators pay only lip-service to the notion.

By the time I had reached high school, the idea of getting a formal education was of no interest to me. I often wondered, to myself and aloud, when I would use the ridiculous information the establishment insisted on ramming down my throat (in fact, I rarely use anything that I learned in school, and this continues to make me wonder whether we are really teaching our high school students the right things at all). The point of school was a mystery to me, and the idea that the other students of my age were getting an education that would be helpful in the future eluded me completely. By the time I reached tenth or eleventh grade, I had decided that my days were more usefully spent alone in the woods. Being bored, wet and lonely was a more attractive option than going to school. At least I could get through the day without being reprimanded, and sometimes I managed to persuade a friend to join me in the woods so that we could be bored and wet together. It does not sound like a lot of fun, does it? Well, it often was not. But it beat the hell out of another day in the classroom.

One day, I was skipping school with my two closest friends, Jimmy and Doug. We were smoking a joint, as most middle-class kids did whenever they could back in the late sixties. It was about ten thirty in the morning, and we were headed for a place called World's End – a large meadow overlooking the Atlantic Ocean. It was a beautiful spot, which could have been designed as a backdrop to getting high. Now, I was never very lucky about breaking the rules and getting away with it, and this day was no exception. Just as I took a deep hit on the joint, Mom drove down the road towards us. She saw us and screeched to a furious halt.

"Why aren't you in school?" she screamed. With the quick wit of an impulsive manipulator, I looked her straight in the eyes and told her that we were on our way to the elementary school to help teach the children how to read. As if I would *ever* have been chosen to be a tutor. I *don't* think so! Initially, Mom seemed to buy the story. I couldn't believe it. For the first time ever, she had swallowed one of my tall tales. Or so I thought.

"That's great, boys," she said, with a knowing look in her eye. "I'll drive you there so that you don't have to walk so far."

What could we do but accept? Once we arrived at the elementary school, we thanked her politely for the ride, left the car and entered a building we had never been in before. Once inside, we dashed madly for an exit, and burst out the back, laughing wildly. Mom's attempt to call our bluff had not paid off. Instead, we called hers, and escaped the torment of another endless, meaningless parental lecture on morality.

Although a lot of people still think that lying came naturally to me, it did not. It developed as a means of survival. As a way of escaping from the circumstances that ADHD made hard for me, like school or the trouble that I had created. Of course, lying generates more lying – if it is successful. Why do people tell untruths? There are two reasons. To get what they want, and/or to avoid punishment. When a lie works, the individual has every incentive in the world to tell more lies. Today, working with children and teenagers with ADHD, my advice to parents and other caregivers is to avoid creating an environment that fosters lies, and thus avoid the reinforcement of the habit. How? It is very easy. Never ask a question unless you already know the answer. Start by saying what you believe: "Richard, it is my opinion that you are skipping school." Then state why you think so: "I think that you are skipping school because it is ten thirty and you are not where you are supposed to be." Finally, state your strategy for dealing with the situation: "You are grounded!"

"What if I am not always right?" you may protest. Well, you may be wrong occasionally, but the truth is that parents know their children well, by and large, and most of the time you are going to be right. Even if you are not, you still deliver the message that if the child is going to do something wrong, he is going to be punished, and would be well-advised to avoid problems or problematic situations in the future. By avoiding environments that foster the telling of lies, future lies are inhibited from developing, and by abstaining from telling untruths, the child will escape punishment in the future. For most parents, the most difficult part of this is probably not asking questions, and simply making presumptive or declarative statements.

The fact is that most parents who have to deal with children who chronically lie want to give them the benefit of the doubt, a chance to be honest when they ask the child a question to which they do not already know the answer. But when this happens, the child is given the opportunity to try to escape punishment or retribution by telling an undetected lie. The child with ADHD quickly learns that there is a price to pay for untethered behavior, and that a lie may make it easier to deal with: "Sure Mom, I was in school today. Of course, I passed the test."

A simple cost/benefit analysis quickly shows that telling a lie is more likely to result in a safe outcome. Of course, the parents say, "If you lie, you will be in even bigger trouble than you are already in." But what the ADHD child hears is " …. trouble … you're … in." Once they have absorbed that message, the choice is easy. To escape punishment, tell as many lies as seem necessary. One might say that the trouble a lie creates is greater than the actual trouble the ADHD behavior caused in the first place, and that therefore it does not pay off. But this analysis is done from the point of view of someone without a disability. The individual with ADHD – and I include myself here – only hears the word "punishment" and his course of action is then predetermined: escape, run, hide, blame. But do not knowingly subject yourself to the resulting putative whim of another.

By the time I reached adolescence I was a master at telling lies. I told untruths to cover up things that I had done, things that

I had not done when I should have and lies just for the heck of it. I knew that it did not matter what I had really done, as I would be judged on what people thought I had done, so I did not have much incentive to be truthful. Inventive fictions and lies which my parents and teachers could not disprove at least gave me a degree of personal satisfaction, and sometimes kept me out of trouble.

This brings us to another matter. Lying, per se, is a symptom of Oppositional Defiant Disorder, and not of ADHD. But it clearly behooves the parent to remember that ODD is a learned disorder, and not a problem founded in genetics. Simply put, the uninhibited ADHD individual is prone to behave in ways that announce that if a problem has occurred they are a good candidate for blame. Being blamed often naturally creates an aversion to the sound of their name being called from afar, facilitating the need for avoidance and thereby the birth of a habitual liar. Punishment potential via high maintenance behavior equals increased probability of avoidance behavior; the lie.

Teenagers with ADHD are immature and have problems with schoolwork, but they experience feelings of romantic love and sexual attraction just as much as their peers do. Maybe even more, because they are not able to stand back from their feelings and analyze them to any extent. I had many crushes on girls over the years, but the first time I was really love-struck was when I got to know Wendy in tenth grade. She was everything I had ever wanted; beautiful, fun, smart, entertaining … and way out of my league. Or so I felt. Wendy was the archetypal living doll, with an hourglass figure, blond hair, large blue eyes and a face like an angel. And I was the scum of the earth. I was not even worthy of a glance from such a goddess. I would gladly have thrown myself on the ground before her so that she could avoid getting her feet wet in a puddle, if I had thought that it might help, but I knew that Wendy could never consider a boy like me as her equal, much less as someone she might actually grow to like and go out with.

Actually, I was popular with the girls in my class – considered a "good catch" – but I could never believe it, so convinced was I of my inferiority. Whenever a girl looked at me flirtatiously or made a flattering remark, my immediate reaction was to assume that she was making fun. Why would a pretty girl like *me*, for goodness' sake? I was a stupid, clumsy klutz. Everyone knew that! If a girl did like me enough to want to go out with me, then there must be something wrong with her.

As a psychologist, I often see teenagers with identical feelings of rejection and inferiority – even if they have scores of friends and admirers of the opposite sex. By the time they reach their teenage years, they have completely internalized the idea that they are unlikable, irredeemably clumsy, stupid, awkward and unloved. If a pretty girl or handsome boy shows interest, they are sure that it is all a cruel joke, or will demean themselves in order to hang on to the affection they are shown. In girls especially, this can take the form of agreeing to sexual relations with anyone who shows interest, even when they do not want to. When the teenage relationship ends, as they inevitably do, the teen with ADHD is left with the conviction that it failed because of them. Because they did something wrong, because they are stupid, unattractive and bad. A precedent for failing in affectionate and romantic relationships is set from the start, and many people with ADHD will never succeed in breaking the pattern. From now on, they will enter every relationship with the conviction that, sooner or later, they will do something wrong and the object of their love will leave them. With this attitude, that is usually exactly what happens, and ADHD boys and girls alike often adopt what looks on the surface like a cavalier approach to sex and relationships – easy come, easy go – while inside they want nothing more than an affirmation that they are not as worthless and stupid as they believe themselves to be.

For a long time, I admired Wendy from a distance, gazing at her longingly and wistfully imagining what it would be like to be able to walk hand-in-hand with her, share "our song" and do the countless romantic things that I pretended to find lame. But I never dared to do anything about the way I felt. It was better to suffer the pangs of unrequited love than the agonies of rejection.

One day at lunch, I was sitting against a fence when Wendy came and sat beside me. We had spoken before, but never for more than a few moments, or with any depth. On this glorious, never-to-be-forgotten day, we ended up teasing each other, trying to put pieces of straw up each other's nose in a crude but exciting ritual of first contact, which marked the beginning of a life-long friendship and love.

As my friendship developed with Wendy, I became increasingly familiar with her habits and social rituals. One of the rituals that Wendy developed with her friend Jan was a secret code which they used for talking about guys in front of other people without being understood, a sort of whistle. It always gave rise to great peals of laughter, and I was driven crazy by not being able to understand. Eventually, it grew too exasperating to deal with and I demanded to know what the code meant. It was an interesting noise that fascinated me, while at the same time threatening me, because of my inability to decipher the meaning. The shrill whistle was made by inhaling through the lips while at the same time uttering the words "too cute". Whenever they saw a boy they considered desirable, Wendy and Jan did this. When at last Wendy relented and told me the meaning of their secret code, I realized that the girls had been directing their "too cute" signal in the direction of one of my best friends, Brock. Brock!

"What does he have that I don't?" I jealously mused. The answer was not hard to find: "He's not a stupid klutz, like me. That's what he's got that I don't. Of course Wendy likes him more than you." Brock was oblivious of what was going on, of course, and I did not go out of my way to enlighten him. It was bad enough knowing that Wendy thought he was cute; it would be terrible if he knew it too, and decided to ask her out!

Although we were at my house, and Wendy was there because she was my friend, I instantly began to question whether Wendy cared for me as I did for her. "*Is she just using me to get near to Brock?*" Now, I know that Wendy did think of me as one of her favorites, but at the time her adoration of Brock clearly signaled to me that I was sub-standard, a lesson that I had internalized too many times to count by then. Despite my feelings of dejection, I managed to focus on my desire to have Wendy in my life and simply continued the pursuit of the love that seemed light years away.

"Why not me?" was my lonely cry. All teens meet some rejection in love, but Wendy's apparent indifference to my silent adoration really hurt me badly, because it seemed to confirm the lesson I had been taught from early childhood. I was bad, stupid, unlikable and unlovable. Of course no beautiful girl would ever want a worm like me. I had been stupid to even imagine that one could or would, especially a girl as beautiful and talented as this one, Wendy.

But Wendy did like me, at least a little, and we became involved. We did not "go steady", except for two weeks once when, as fate would have it, Wendy was in a motorcycle accident, and lost one of her big toes, which left her with mobility problems for a while. I jumped at the chance to drive her around and have her all to myself. But she always came back to me, after breaking my heart again and again, every time she went out with another boy. Wendy remained a touchstone throughout my adolescence and early adulthood, and we still communicate even now.

Throughout those last years in high school – before my premature departure – parties played a big part in all the students' lives. We were young, full of raging hormones and old enough to drive and go out by ourselves. The world belonged to us. It was time for the old people to move over.

Whenever the opportunity arose, all the kids headed out to a local lake, Trip Hammer Pond, to spend the night dancing, drinking, getting high and making out. I was always there too, but I hovered on the edge of the festivities clutching the cans of extra-strength beer which I needed to drink to give myself the courage to join the fray. While I was still sober, I would stand and stare at the activities and wonder how other people knew how to approach each other, chat and laugh. How they were able to enjoy themselves without being crushed by feelings of inferiority. How they just knew how to interact with each other and have fun, as if it were the most natural thing in the world. The process eluded me completely, until my ingrained feelings of worthlessness had been numbed by beer.

But by the time I had more alcohol than blood in my veins, I was the life and soul of the party, dancing, picking up girls and getting wilder and crazier by the moment. I needed the alcohol to help me to forget who I "really" was – Dick the failure, the no-hoper, the guy that everyone expected to see pumping gas for the rest of his life after flunking out of school. Alcohol and drugs helped me to feel momentarily like the guy I *wished* I was; charismatic, smart, fun and above all, in control of myself – in an out-of-control sort of way. When I was high, no-one could stop me from soaring. I could be anyone I wanted to be, or so I fondly imagined until the effects of the alcohol and drugs wore off and normal life resumed itself, along with a thumping headache.

Another way I compensated for my feelings of worthlessness was by paying almost obsessive attention to my clothes, even by the anxious standards of the typical teenager. I had to be *cool*, at all costs. Sure, most teenagers are preoccupied with fashion, but as in most things, I was way out on the extreme end of the equation. As one of the first local hippies, I was constantly preoccupied with concerns as to whether my bell-bottoms were wide enough, or too wide. Were they frayed the right way? Did they look casually well-worn, or just shabby? How could I tell, anyway? Were my tie-die shirts too dark, or too light? Too patterned, or not patterned enough? Did I look alright, or did I stand out? *Could people tell that I was different?* I paraded in front of the mirror in the bedroom, not like a peacock strutting my stuff, but in an anxious quest to see if I could somehow make myself look right. Perhaps, if I could manage that, the rest would follow. Fashion became a sort of shell, protecting me from the stares and accusations of authority figures and peers who intimidated me with their air of confidence: "They aren't looking at me. They're looking at my clothes …"

I remember a party at my friend Brock's house, when I was sixteen years old. It was a typical party; we were smoking all the usual drugs, consuming vast quantities of beer and generally having a pretty good time, according to the hippie standards of the day. Then a great idea struck me. I was wearing my orange platform shoes (don't laugh, please – I was not the only one wearing ridiculous clothes in those days). *Obviously*, I should go streaking! I tore off all my clothes, stood up in nothing but those ludicrous shoes (now privately dubbed my "streaking shoes"), and entered the main party room. In general, streakers were supposed to dash through crowds so quickly that nobody could see anything but a glimpse of flesh (hence the name), but this idea seemed so dull that I carefully paused for long enough to take in the reactions of my peers. I wanted to be sure that I was living up to their expectations.

"What are you doing, Dickie?" an attractive female friend named Terry asked, looking at me in bemusement over her can of beer.

"I'm going streaking!" I proclaimed proudly, and rushed out the front door of the house into a miserable, wet September night. I was back in fifteen minutes with my entire right side covered in blood and wet earth, and Terry asked, "What the Hell happened?"

Again, I paused for dramatic effect, and told her, "I wiped out."

By the time I reached my late teens, my interest in pot-smoking had prompted me to plant a crop on the roof of our home. Why spend my allowance on pot when I could grow my own? And the roof of our family home was just perfect for the job. Except for one little thing. It was not exactly a million miles away from my Mom and Dad. But I did not let a detail like that worry me. I was looking forward to a good harvest, and to being able to get high and distribute free pot to my friends and the people I wanted to like me. Then, Dad decided to visit the roof for some reason, and came across the potted plants. With a roar, he threw them from the roof to the yard, narrowly missing me as I walked by! I was a typical, difficult, ADHD youth, and he was a typical, difficult, ADHD father, with a temper as short as his attention span and only slightly longer than the length of time his work contracts usually lasted. In retrospect, this episode is as funny as it is painful. At the time, we both felt full of justifiable anger. I had "confirmed" to him that I was a wastrel, a spendthrift, lazy boy who just wanted to lie back and get high at his expense. He, on the other hand, had shown me how "lame and conservative and boring" he was. One of my brothers took me aside later that day, when things had cooled down somewhat.

"Why didn't you just plant the pot somewhere else?" he asked. "There are a thousand places where Dad would never have found them!"

"I didn't think of that," was my honest reply. I had not thought beyond the realization that the roof was the perfect place for my horticultural endeavors.

Things were not great with Mom, either. I even reached a low point when I pushed her in anger, and she fell over. I do not even recall exactly why I became so angry, but I remember the hot rush of emotion propelling my arm to reach out violently and shove her narrow shoulder so hard that she topped over onto the driveway. I loved my mother and never, ever wanted to hurt her, but my level of frustration took over and I just pushed harder than I had intended. She fell awkwardly onto the hard ground and lay there for a moment, stunned by the shock of the fall and the horror of the realization that her youngest son had just knocked her over, apparently with a degree of cold deliberation that was truly shocking.

I still remember the horror I felt as I looked at Mom struggling up from where she had landed on the ground and realized what I had done. I had committed the ultimate sin of raising my hand in anger against that most sacred of all beings, Mother. I had made Mom fall and hurt herself. Not even the lowest of lowlifes pushes or hits his own mother! Now I knew that I really had gone about as low as anybody can. My stammered apologies made little impact on Mom, who rose shakily to her feet and, raising her arm as if she thought that I were about to strike, reentered the house.

"Don't, Dickie," she said. "Just don't." She was too upset to listen to anything I had to say, and I had rendered myself almost speechless with shock at my own expression of the clumsy anger I had felt.

Incidents like this distressed Mom enormously, as she had no way of understanding that the violent act was born out of raw emotion, not intention. Another day, I found her in tears, holding her face in her hands and sobbing in sheer desperation. Now, Mom was really the pillar of our family, the one who kept us all together and took care of everyone, including Dad. She was definitely not the sort of person to sit and cry about the slightest little thing, so I knew that something had upset her very, very badly. I moved to try and comfort her, patting her awkwardly on the shoulder with adolescent gracelessness: "Mom, is there anything I can …?"

When she felt my hand, Mom looked up at me bitterly, wiping her tears away with the back of her hand and said, "If I could take back the long hours of labor that I went through to have you, I would do it in an instant. There's nothing you can do. You've done more than enough already. Just go away."

Her words hit me full on and I could actually feel my heart contract with the pain of her rejection. I withdrew my hand and my attempts to comfort and left the room without another word. Only the slam of the door behind me hinted at my desolation.

No-one, of any age, should have to hear from their mother that they should never have been born. The fact that our gentle, loving Mom said those awful words shows how difficult the situation had become for us both. My untreated ADHD did not hurt only me. It came perilously close to destroying our relationship forever.

When I was around sixteen, after years of trying and failing to cope with my complex needs and apparent lack of any interest in work or responsibility, Mom and Dad came to the conclusion that they should send me away to boarding school, thinking that a change of environment would help and also – although they might not have wanted to admit it – reveling in the thought of the blissful peace that would reign without me in the house.

As a psychologist, I often meet parents who have reached the stage whereby they just want to shrug off their difficult child and get on with life without him (sometimes, boarding school does help, providing the young person with a change of scene and a structured environment). Do not suppose that they reach this stage quickly. For the parents of an ADHD child, it is a long, painful journey from early childhood to the realization that they just cannot cope any more. Together with their child, they have been through failed grades, a childhood without real friends, painful accident after painful accident, rejection by peers, teachers and siblings, expulsion from school … the list goes on and on. The point at which Mom and Dad feel that they have to say "good bye" to their child for his own good is reached only by struggling to survive trauma for years. It is an admission of failure.

So off I went to Brewster Academy, a strict boarding school located in the middle of nowhere. I was miserable without Wendy, and begged her to send me letters sprayed with the perfume she used to wear, so that I could smell her as I read them, and use them for comfort. I remember falling asleep with the paper crumpled beneath my nose, desperately trying to inhale Wendy's scent (I still remember the name of the perfume, Clear Spruce Sweden) and pretending that I was at home, where the rules may have been ludicrous and impossible not to break, but were at least familiar. Boarding school did not last for long. I already knew it was not going to work out, no matter what I did, so I kicked back, drank beer and waited to get into trouble. Actually, I *wanted* to get into trouble. Trouble would be my ticket home. When it came, I was ready. Some roommates and I were found with alcohol in our room, and I took full responsibility for every single can. Not because I wanted to save their hides, but because I knew that this was a way out. I had had enough. I called Wendy that night, and she came up with a couple of friends from home and brought me back. Dad was angry, and Mom just looked at me, too tired to respond, but if looks could kill, I would have been dead a dozen times over.

It was back to the local high school for me, and the usual litany of failures and complaints. But at least I was at home, and at least I had my friends, and Wendy. Wendy was always there for me.

Shortly after I came home from Brewster academy, Mom and Dad announced that we were moving to Franklin, New Hampshire, where Dad would find another job. I was horrified, but despite my protests, once again friends would be left behind. This time, I was leaving Wendy to live in a town that I was sure would be filled with nothing but rednecks and hillbillies. Who else would want to live somewhere like that? Dad had lost his job … again! He was always successful in work, but no job ever lasted for longer than three years. The same impulsivity that is my burden (and my unadulterated pleasure, at times) was also his. He had a short temper, found it next to impossible to follow company policy and always wound up having problems with colleagues, bosses or employees.

The Kuendigs moved home, yet again, and I was to finish high school in yet another town. By now, I drank a pint of whiskey most mornings before school, to give myself the courage to get through the day. It was too late for a fresh start, and the usual round of punishment, detention and suspension was soon underway. School was no better in the new town than it had been before, and within a matter of days, I was identified as an established troublemaker, and duly punished. Anyway, one day I was given detention yet again, for one infraction or another, probably for something to do with not going to gym class – ever. I did not want to stay in school a minute longer than I had to, so I packed up and went home without serving even a second of the detention that the school so self-righteously felt I deserved. Bear in mind that at this time I was a young man of seventeen – old enough to get married, should I have wanted to. One year away from being old enough to join the army and die for my country. ADHD or no ADHD, should I still have been treated like a child? I don't think so.

Back at the house, the phone rang and I answered. It was the school principal, calling to inform my parents that I had skipped detention and, yet again, was in trouble. After all these years, I do not remember the man's name, but I can assure you that he was the antithesis of me. He was old, and I was young. He was bald, and I was a long-haired hippy. He represented the establishment, and I was anti-establishment. He was completely uptight, and I was all in favor of the love, peace and free sex of the late sixties and, by now, the early seventies. I hated him, and my sentiments were warmly returned.

"Dick," he said. "I want to speak to your mother."

"No," I answered, without hesitating.

"What do you mean, 'no'? Put your mother on right away!"

"I'm afraid that isn't going to be possible, " I told him in the same indignant tones that he was using. I was beginning to enjoy myself. It was fun being in a position of authority for a change.

"I demand to speak to your mother!"

"Well, I demand that you stop demanding."

"Young man, if you continue like this, you'll be in even more trouble than you are already in!"

"Oh, yeah? Do you think I give a fuck …

Things were progressing nicely when Mom picked up the extension in another room. She was far from delighted, if unsurprised, to hear about all the detentions I had been getting and my performance on the phone was the icing on the cake. She sent me back down to school where the principal summoned me to his office to read me the riot act. Boy, was he mad. Before I had even closed the door behind me, he was yelling. He turned red right to the very top of his bald head. The veins pulsed on his neck, and he probably could have been heard in the next county. I sat and listened for ten minutes or so, while he gradually lost control even further, making *me* the calm one for a change.

Take into consideration that, by now, my entire life had been filled with teachers, school counselors, assistant principals and even Mr. Fallon from Hingham, none of whom had hesitated to tell me that I was "worthless". I had come to understand that the word "worthless" was my special epitaph, my scarlet letter. It belonged to me. More than once, Mr. Fallon had appointed himself prophet, and said that I was "worthless and headed nowhere" and should therefore "just quit school now and stop wasting both our time."

When, after thirteen years (don't forget that I repeated first grade) of being told that I was useless, I heard this bald-headed loon scream, "Why don't you leave school right now? You're a useless nothing, you've always been a useless nothing, you'll always *be* a useless nothing and nobody wants anything to do with you. Why don't you just get the hell out of my school? You'll be lucky if you get a job as a garbage man! Who do you think you are, walking in here and behaving as if you didn't have to answer to anybody?" I had had enough. I stood up, looked him dead in the eye and answered his screams with calm and even a sort of dignity.

"Fuck you," I told him calmly. "You know what? You win. I quit." And I left. I was seventeen years old. It was not the first time that I had been advised to leave school, " … because you're never going to amount to anything anyway," but I certainly wanted it to be the last. I did not need to take that sort of abuse from anybody. I was ready to face the world on my own. Or so I thought.

Boy, did I have a surprise.

Back at the house, I told Mom that I had left school for good and that I was leaving home. I cooked up a plan to find a plumber and become his apprentice. I did not know anything about plumbing, and I had never met a plumber, but I had heard that they made pretty good money – a cousin of mine was making a good living as a plumber at that time – and that sounded good to me. I would have everything I needed then. Money to spend on parties and drugs and good times, my independence, and the respect of my peers. I had not quite thought out how I would go about finding a plumber and persuading him to take me on, but I was sure that it would not prove too difficult.

Mom blanched when I told her the news. She knew, if I did not, that my idea was not a good one, and visions of all the trouble I could cause myself flashed through her head. If I did manage to make some money, I would spend it on drugs. Would I wind up taking an accidental overdose? Would she learn that I had died only when the cops knocked on the door? If I didn't – which was more likely – how was I going to make a living? Stealing? Selling drugs for some shady pusher? I looked like a young man, but she knew that in a lot of ways, I was still a little boy on the inside, and the thought of seeing me trying to make my way in the world was like having to imagine leaving a toddler in the middle of a city and waiting for him to make his own way home. She was right to be worried.

The problem was that I had absolutely no idea how I would carry the plan out. AHDH had played a dirty trick on me again. The outcome of the idea was as clear as could be, but I lacked any planning at all. Where would I find a plumber looking for an apprentice? Where would I live while I was learning my trade? There was no method whatsoever behind my ideas. Sure, it was impulsive, but at the time, it sounded good. I imagined the generous wage packet and the freedom but never quite got around to thinking about acquiring the training.

That very day, I left home. School was out forever, and there was no reason for me to stick around in a place that I considered to be a tedious backwater. I went back to Hingham, the town where I had spent the early and middle years of my adolescence. The town where Wendy lived. I had a car, I had a tent, I had some clothes, and I had forty dollars in my pocket. The world was my magic carpet, and nothing was going to stand in my flight.

It was good to be back in Hingham, but what was I going to do with no home and nowhere to sleep? I had been sure that my friends would support me in the manner to which I was accustomed (a song I often hear from teenage patients in my office); yet another impulsive assumption that turned out to be entirely false. How could they, even if they wanted to? They were kids, still living with their parents. And why would their parents want to take on someone else's teenage son, a known trouble-maker and high school drop-out? You can imagine the scenario.

For a few weeks, I parked my car in the forest, slept in the back seat and went to my girlfriend Karen's house [6] in the mornings, where I took a shower before she went to school. After a few weeks, Karen's Mom took pity on me and said that I could sleep in the upper story of their barn, where there was a bed and a place for me to leave my clothes. It was good for a while. But after a few weeks of being awoken by the horse, which lived right below me, it just got to be too much. Why? Well, let's put it this way … the startling noises and pungent odor that came from downstairs as the horse greeted every morning by breaking wind, defecating and urinating like the Niagara falls lost their rustic appeal pretty quickly. A man has to have his standards, and I could not go on living above an equine toilet indefinitely. What if I had wanted to entertain? There is no way I could have brought my friends back to my home when it was, quite literally, a barn.

---

[4] You probably thought I was going to say 'Wendy's house', but by then Wendy and I knew that although we loved each other deeply, our relationship timing was way off. If I was available she wasn't and if she was I wasn't.

A little way down the street, another friend, Sharon, lived. There was a forest behind her house, and I pitched my tent there just as soon as the weather got warm enough. Even a tent was better than sharing my sleeping quarters with a horse!

Sharon used to let me into the house after her parents went to work so that I could wash and grab something to eat, and I was pretty happy about the situation, for as long as it lasted. My little camping ground became the center of plenty of impromptu parties, as old friends from school turned up to hand out, drink, smoke pot and have a good time before heading back to their parents' houses and their warm, cozy beds. Some of them said that they envied me. I did not have to get up early and go to school. Nobody told me what to do. But the truth of the matter was that I was the one who envied them. They did not seem to have to struggle to maintain a good relationship with their parents and, although they may have hated school, they managed to put in the hours and make the grade. All talents which had eluded me for my whole life.

One night, I woke up to find that my tent had vanished. Instead of lying snuggly under the canvas, I was flat on my back on the damp grass, looking up at the stars. I turned groggily to my friend Rick, who lay beside me, surrounded by empty beer cans and cigarette papers, and asked, "What the fuck?" I vaguely remembered having crawled into my sleeping bag the night before, but anything that happened after that was a blur. We had been drinking, as usual.

"You were on fire last night," Rick told me, pulling himself up on his elbow. "The tent went up, you went up … we had to pull you out. You could have died, man!" He seemed quite excited about the whole thing.

"Holy shit!" I exclaimed, sinking back down into my sleeping bag. "On fire. And I didn't even notice."

I had passed out in the tent after indulging in too many drinks and drugs, but now all of my possessions and my home were gone and, once again, I had nowhere to live. What was I going to do? Where was I supposed to go now? I certainly was not going to go back to live in a stable with a horse, and returning to my parents' house was not an option.

"What the hell," I told myself. "Something will turn up." And it did. As luck would have it, I encountered a man throwing out a refrigerator box later that very day as I walked down Main Street, and I knew that fate was throwing me a crumb.

"Can I have that?" I asked him excitedly.

He shrugged. "Sure, I don't care. I was throwing it out, anyway." He did not seem to wonder why an eager, long-haired teenager wanted his old refrigerator box.

"Great, thanks!" I dragged my find back to the woods. With the addition of a plastic tarpaulin I had picked up from the trash outside a department store I had a new home for the next six months. My box and me were going to be just fine.

Not once during those difficult months did I think of calling home. And to the best of my knowledge, my parents had no idea where I was and did nothing to try to find out. It seemed that we had pretty much given up on each other (the fact that they were still holding out for me was not clear until years later), but they probably would not have been all that surprised to learn that I was living in a box. They were not surprised by anything I did by this stage, and never doubted that every decision I made was deliberate, based on whatever crazy logic they thought that I subscribed to. I was – and still am, in a way – the black sheep of the family.

My forty dollars did not last long, and I could not depend on friends for all of my food, so I became expert in stealing steak from one of the stores in town, and lived on nothing but meat for months on end. I did get a job for a while, as a "petroleum transfer engineer," as I liked to call my new role as a gas-pumper. It lasted for all of two days. Then I tried working in a smoke detector factory for a while, on the advice of a friend, Jimmy. He had been able to cope with the tedium of a menial factory job, but routine work is not suited to a teen with ADHD, and I did not stick it out for more than a few days before packing it in.

I did not do everything wrong, though. I did take the High School equivalency test, and passed it, because I knew I would never find employment without a diploma. What does it say for the American educational system when a drop-out who flunked almost every grade can get an equivalency diploma so easily? Was I smart, or does our school system have some major flaws? Both, probably. Passing that exam without ever having read a book was a vindication of the intelligence I knew I had, even though I failed at everything I tried my hand at. I knew that I was smart, I had the paper-work to prove it, but still, things did not come together for me. I went right on living in a box on a diet consisting exclusively of steak, pot and alcohol. And it was a lot less fun every day.

I was constantly amazed to find how wet things can get just from dew in the air. Cardboard boxes should have health warnings printed on the side: "Living here is dangerous for your health." No matter how hard you try to waterproof them, the damp and cold always get in. You just cannot live in a box for months on end and stay healthy. Eventually, living rough made me ill, and even though my friend Sharon was letting me into her house to wash and eat, I had to do something. I called home: "Hi? Hello, it's me, Dick …"

"No," my parents said, before even hearing what I had to say. "We don't want you to come here with all the trouble that brings with it."

"But I'm not well, can I just …"

"Can't you see a doctor there? What do you need to come here for? Are we only good to fall back on when you get into trouble?" They had had enough of me and the hurt that I always seemed to end up causing. I had never been diagnosed as having a disability of any kind, and there was never a suggestion that my behavior was anything other than a choice, calculated to destroy my own life and make theirs a misery. Their immediate reaction to my thought of coming home was to push me away and, bearing in mind that they had no concept of what ADHD was, let alone a disability perspective, I cannot blame them. I had hurt them badly and even then, I was aware of this. After a few days, however, they relented, and told me that I should come home. The night before I left, a friend of mine, Mike, smashed my car up, and I made it back to Mom and Dad's house despite the fact that it was pretty much falling apart, as was I.

On the brink of adulthood, it had never occurred to me or anybody else that I might have a developmental disability. Other people thought that all of the fault of my behavior lay with me, and so far as I was concerned, it was the world's problem. I could find no correspondence between the way I saw and experienced things and the way other people did. What was wrong? Why couldn't people just accept me the way I was? And why did I still keep getting into trouble? The answers to my questions remained elusive and I continued to live for the moment. I got better, physically, and moved out of home again.

Settled into an apartment with a number of other young men, parties, drinking and drugs continued to be an important part of my life. I loved to get high, and remember that, in those days, everyone smoked pot. Along with casual sex and long hair, it was a crucial element of the zeitgeist of those heady days. We never really took seriously the fact that taking drugs was still illegal, thus precipitating our arrest and prosecution. It was bound to happen sooner or later. We made no secret of our habits, and eventually the local cops decided that enough was enough.

The police trashed our apartment as they searched for the drugs, slashing their way through mattresses and pillows, emptying cans of beer into our beds, and generally causing gleeful havoc. When Mom heard that the drugs were finally found in the freezer, her comment was, "Trust Richard not to be able to find a good hiding place." Yet again, I was in trouble with authority.

9
Lessons Learned

In my day, ADHD was rarely mentioned, if at all. In the more recent past, ADHD was thought of as a "childhood ailment" and it was assumed that no treatment would be needed for adolescents and adults. Consequently, many people with ADHD were undiagnosed, or treatment was withdrawn when they reached adolescence and found themselves more vulnerable than ever before.

Now we know that, although symptoms may be slightly different in the older individual with ADHD (for example, unacted upon feelings of restlessness and wanting to wander about rather than actually doing so), they are still present. In fact, adolescence is an especially delicate stage in the life of the individual with ADHD. Treatments that worked in childhood may not work as well now as they did before, and there is often a lot of pressure on the teen to stop taking medication. This pressure can come in the form of peers who tease, internal feelings of being manipulated and more. Furthermore, the untreated, unmanaged ADHD teen represents a greatly increased risk to his own well-being, and to the well-being of those around him. He is big, he is strong, he is impulsive and he often (about 65% of the time) has a full-blown case of Oppositional Defiant Disorder. If he did not receive the help he needed when he was still a child, it is a lot more difficult to help him now.

On the face of it, the situation for ADHD teenagers is bleak. My ADHD was undiagnosed, but my Mom was right to be horrified when I left school and told her my unworkable plans. Youths with ADHD tend to suffer more with problems of self-esteem, alcoholism, drug abuse and learning problems than other teens. Many drop out of school, experience car accidents and worse. In fact, by some estimates, people with ADHD are *400 percent* more likely to be in a car accident that their same age peers. Let me say that again. People with ADHD are 400 percent more likely to be in a car accident than their same age peers.

Rates of teen suicide are much higher than among the unaffected population and, overall, ADHD teens are much, much more likely than their peers to become seriously injured or to die in the course of their everyday activities, making ADHD a major contributing factor to death among the young. I could easily have inadvertently killed myself a thousand times over in my teenage years. The episode when I nearly went up in flames is just one example among many.

The good news is that all of the above can be helped or even avoided with a proper understanding of the condition and how it works, and responsible treatment and approaches to the disorder. For example, it might be well advised not to allow the ADHD sixteen year old to drive, even though the law (in most states) says they are ready to do so. Remember, ADHD is a developmental disability and one must maintain a disability perspective when making decisions that might have long lasting consequences such as death in an automobile accident. To be forewarned is to be forearmed.

All teens have to struggle with their self-identification as a person who is almost adult, and the realities of life, in which they are still young, still dependent and still in need of help. There probably is not an adolescent in the world who has not entertained fantasies of moving away and living with friends, but reality usually kicks in at some point in the mind of the non-ADHD teen. I often meet ADHD teens who tell me, "I can't take living with my parents any more. I'm going to go and live with my friends. They understand what I am going through." For their own sake, I have to laugh: "Get a grip on reality! Your friends are kids! They can't give you a place to live. Who is going to support you? What are you going to eat? Do you really think you can hold down a job? Even if your

Mom and Dad make you angry, do you honestly think that you can survive without their support?" When I was in their position, even my best friends eventually grew angry with me for living off their families' generosity, and started calling me "leech" and "sponge". Like them, I simply had no realistic concept of how to provide for myself outside the safety of the family environment.

Things are better for ADHD children and teens than they used to be, but that is not to say that life is not hellish any more for far too many. Nobody wants to acknowledge that ADHD is a disability. People with ADHD *cannot* choose to behave and react as other people do and that is especially true for ADHD teens. They have ADHD all the time, and have to work against it every minute of every hour of every day. It never goes away. They are disabled people, even if they do have all their limbs. I am constantly amazed by parents and educators who think that, merely by saying, "Why aren't you more responsible?" to ADHD teens, they will somehow make them realize the error of their ways. ADHD teens would *love* to be more responsible. They do not enjoy standing out and being the constant brunt of jokes and the object of ridicule and punishment. It is no fun bringing home report card after report card with nothing but Fs, and becoming known as the dumb kid in the class, or being the child who is always compared unfavorably to older – or what is worse, younger – siblings. They are not more responsible, because they *cannot* be, period, end of story. They are simply unable to maintain the effort required and this is *not* a fact that is debatable.

By the time many people with ADHD reach their teens, they have acquired a firmly rooted and entirely irrational belief system about themselves, their family, their peers and their place in the world. This is especially true of people who were untreated or inadequately treated for the disability throughout childhood. It might be surprising to the outsider to learn that most ADHD sufferers find it very difficult to let go of the irrational beliefs that they have acquired, and that many are deeply resistant to doing so (this is also true of the individual who is diagnosed in adulthood). A firmly held belief in one's inherent inferiority, lack of intelligence and social gracelessness does not sound like something to cling to but, for many people, any identity is preferable to none. The adolescent may prefer to see himself as the class rebel and entertainer rather than having to wonder about why he finds schoolwork difficult, and start thinking about taking responsibility for his own actions. In fact, just today (May 6, 2003), I spoke to a teenager who is miserably behind in his school work. He told me that he wants to do the work that is due, but that he has ignored the work for so long that he doesn't think he is able to tackle the job, which has grown out of all proportion in his mind. His mother told me that, for the last three years, he has been the class clown and has gone out of his way to avoid work. As an example, she told me that when he was unable to read his assignments, she would read them for him. However, during her reading, he would become so irritating that she admitted having thrown the book at him the very first time she tried to help.

The thought of tackling a range of symptoms resulting from a disability may just seem too difficult to even contemplate. In order for the adolescent – or adult – to become enabled to recognize their disability and move beyond it, they need to learn first how to discard the irrational ideas that they have developed over the years as a sort of protective shell.

Although the dosage may be different, the same medication used to treat children with ADHD can also be useful for adolescents. Parents often express concern that teenagers who receive prescription medication for ADHD may drift easily into taking other drugs, legal and illegal, for recreational purposes. These concerns are understandable, but the research shows that teens who are prescribed and take medication for ADHD are less likely to take drugs than those who should be medicated and are not, probably because the reasons behind the attraction to drugs – an inability to function in the family and school environments and the resulting lack of confidence, inability to delay gratification, behavioral disinhibition, etc. – are being temporarily managed. That said, physicians and other caregivers should not blithely dispense prescription drugs to teenagers without carefully exploring whether or not the medication is really necessary. Teenagers who have been on medication since childhood often express rebellion or a sense of independence by ceasing to take the drug, and this can cause huge problems if their ADHD has not also been treated by using a wide range of non-medical techniques. In fact, some estimates suggest that as many as 85 to 90% of all teenagers with ADHD refuse to take medication when they reach adolescence. They may be expressing their need for independence or rejecting the feeling that they are somehow "different" if they take medication and worry that their peers will find out and brand them as "psycho" or "crazy". Whatever the reason, there are other perils, too. In my office, I often encounter teens who have decided that they would prefer to sell their medication than to take it. Remember that most of the medications for ADHD are stimulants of the central nervous system, and can be abused – there is another name for central nervous system stimulants: Speed. Furthermore, while medication can help to control symptoms, it does not cure anything, and can encourage teachers and parents to rely completely on the drug without making efforts to help the teen develop a more positive way of living. This leaves the teenager, once off medication, experiencing all the same behavioral problems as before. But now, he or she is adult-sized, with adult desires and feelings and strength and the physical and emotional consequences of impulsivity are far, far greater.

All teenagers have to learn how to play the game of life, according to the rules that are already there. Sure, society is flawed, but one lone adolescent kicking against the reins is not going to change anything, and they will need to conform to a large extent. This is a difficult challenge for all adolescents, and much more so for ADHD teens whose every instinct is to fight and kick against the rules. Punishment does not work very well, but reward can. If adolescents understand that acceptable behavior on their part will be rewarded by increased freedom, they are usually much more willing to comply: "Do you want your curfew extended? Then you have to manage not to lose your temper with your siblings." "Do you want an increased allowance? You can have it, if you do not complain about your chores for a week."

ADHD adolescents have to learn how to be respectful, but adults also have to recognize a need for flexibility on their part. If strict rules and punishment are not working – try something else. How long do you go on beating a nail with a crooked hammer before you give up and use a different tool? Parents should never forget that, while adolescents are immature and needy (especially in the case of adolescents with ADHD), they are not children. If they are ever to learn how to function in an adult world, they need to be given some freedom and room to experiment. Unfortunately, because the individual with ADHD has demonstrated a long history of immaturity and impulsivity, most parents actively resist giving them increased freedom. Repeatedly, I have observed that mothers of children with ADHD tend to maintain their rules and regulations in an attempt to control and provide security long into adolescence and even early adulthood. In the mother's eyes, their child – now a budding adult – is still inclined to make weak, impulsive decisions and needs continuous, ongoing guidance. Otherwise, she reasons, they will fall prey to the very forces of society that she has been warning the child about for years. In judging her adolescent child to be immature, mothers of ADHD kids are often completely correct, but by denying them to opportunity to make their own mistakes, learn from them and move on, they are inhibiting their acquiring a sense of maturity. As every parent eventually concludes, there are times when you have to sit back and let mistakes occur. You can not live your child's life for him indefinitely. Provide support and guidance, for sure, but do not aspire to absolute control.

When small children are brought to a physician or psychologist for help with a behavioral disorder, the caregiver expects that parents will be responsible for monitoring the child's progress, administering medication, communicating with teachers and providing feedback to the therapist. All of this would simply be beyond the capabilities of a child in grade school. However, as the patient enters and lives through adolescence he must and should become an active participant in his own treatment program. If not, he will – not unreasonably – feel that medicine and behavior modification techniques are being "done to him", or imposed upon him against his will, and he is likely to begin to resist treatment, reject medication and resent parents and caregivers as interfering adults who do not understand what he is going through, do not respect his autonomy and do not recognize the fact that he is no longer a child but an adult in the making. A sensible psychologist or physician will expect the adolescent patient to begin providing his own feedback about his experiences at school, at home and with his peers (while these may be supplemented with parental feedback). He can, and should, begin to be responsible for taking his own medication, and start working more actively with the adults in his life to coordinate chores, homework and other responsibilities. While ADHD teens are markedly less mature than non-ADHD teens, it is an offense to them, and a positive handicap to their developing a sensible, adult approach to their disability to continue treating them as if they were small children throughout their adolescent years.

By the time most ADHD kids reach their teens, they have come to think of themselves as being congenitally flawed, bad people. They have grown used to the bad report cards, the criticism of teachers and other adult authority figures and the jeers and taunts of their peers. ADHD adolescents tend to try to compensate for all of this by striving to be popular and accepted. They are extremely susceptible to advertising which tells them that they just *have* to have a certain product (clothes item, cosmetic product, sports paraphernalia) if they are to be accepted and can sometimes beg, borrow or steal in their quest for the latest "cool" product that might help them to look just right and be admired by their classmates. They struggle to win acceptability by becoming the class clown, and by playing up to expectations of them as amusing trouble-makers ("maybe I'm stupid and dumb, but at least I'm funny"). Because they cannot accept who they are – having been categorically taught that they are not good people – they try to construct another identity for themselves ("the one who will do anything for a laugh"). All of the above was certainly true of me, with my obsession for my appearance and my willingness to do almost anything, no matter how foolish, if I thought that it would make people laugh, and like me better.

Some ADHD adolescents succeed in being popular with their peers, but often at the cost of their own sense of self, and at the expense of whatever chance they have left of becoming acceptable in the eyes of their parents and teachers. Having created an image of themselves as the funny-man, it becomes impossible for them to express their serious side, or to confess to occasional feelings of weakness or vulnerability. Ironically, even the most "popular" ADHD teen never truly enjoys his notoriety among his peers. By the time the teenage years are reached, feelings of worthlessness have become so ingrained that he never believes that schoolmates can enjoy his company fully. When they laugh, he is sure that they are laughing at, not with, him. He will probably feel a need to get drunk or high on drugs before he can relax, and he (or she) may become sexually promiscuous in an attempt to gain admiration or approval, something which often backfires with alarming consequences in the case of girls with the condition, who have to struggle with the extra burden of being thought "easy" in a society which applauds male sexuality and still tries to punish its female equivalent.

If we wish all our teens a bright future, we need to learn to allow them to be themselves, and to understand that their own identities are not bad ones. Above all, we can start laying the foundations for a reasonably happy, successful adolescence in childhood, by ensuring that ADHD children obtain the specific behavioral treatment and care they need.

The problems with schoolwork that can negatively influence younger children are still present in teens. Again, school grades do a poor job of reflecting the intelligence and ability of the ADHD teen, who typically has problems with concentration, task completion and academic achievement despite his high or average levels of intelligence. Added to these difficulties are the challenges of simply being an adolescent, with the overwhelming changes in hormonal balance, growth and appearance that this entails. All teenagers experience the urge to rebel, to stand out from the crowd, and to vocalize resentment about perceived injustice. All of this is much more so in the case of the ADHD teen. Problems can be severely exacerbated by teachers or instructors who are unsympathetic to people with ADHD, do not take the condition seriously, and will not make allowances for or adjust classes to pupils with special needs. It is crucial to maintain lines of communication between parents, teachers and teens, and proper education of teachers dealing with ADHD teens is a necessity, not a luxury, although it is almost always lacking.

The educational system can offer a higher degree of flexibility to students at high school level than in grade school, with opportunities to supplement or replace certain classes that may be problematic, as in the case of the teacher who is extremely hostile to ADHD teens, to the extent of verbalizing doubts that the condition exists at all and refusing to make any adjustments to assignment length and time allowed for examinations. However, this flexibility is contingent on the cooperation of the school in question, and this, of course, is often lacking, despite legal recognition of the condition, and the lip service paid to the notion that schools have certain obligations. Too often, a young person's needs for help and flexibility in approaching their education become the object of a power struggle between school management and the family and care providers of ADHD students. A perfect example of this is a recent patient of mine who had/has both ADHD and a diagnosed learning disability.

Last year, Michael was a junior at a local high school named "Jackson". When he began to experience difficulties with an English course, I suggest that he withdraw from the class offered in the school, and take an alternative course via an accredited correspondence program. I could not see the problem. The alternative classes were fully authorized by the state, and the freedom from the regular class would allow Michael to work at his own pace and achieve the results he needed. The school did not react favorably, to put it mildly. You would have sworn that I suggest he assassinate the Pope! Not only did the school authorities refuse to allow Michael to take the correspondence course, they refused to accept the standard test results I provided, which proved that the youth had a learning disability.

"This is absolutely ridiculous," I told Michael and his mother. "I am a qualified, experienced and licensed professional who makes his living diagnosing and treating learning disabilities." Frankly, I was insulted and outraged that the school dared to belittle the qualifications that took me many hard years of study to earn, and the years of experience I have accumulated in exercising my profession. My attempts to reason with the school were fruitless. In fact, the in-school special education coordinator took my suggestions as a personal insult, telling the boy's mother in dismissive tones that, "We know all about Dr. Kuendig's entrepreneurial endeavors, his tutors and the like, and the only testing we accept is that performed by our own school psychologist." Now, this school's actions are not only unethical – they are illegal. The special education coordinator considered her ego and the reputation of the high school to be more important than the educational needs of my patient, Michael. Needs which should have been protected by the law's recognition of ADHD as a developmental disability.

During the course of repeated efforts to find a compromise, Michael's mother was rebuked, insulted and degraded until she was forced not to take the matter any further, for fear that Michael would be the one to suffer retribution on the part of the school administration. Sadly, her fears were not without justification and her decision completely understandable.

Michael was unable to take the correspondence course because of the school's decision to place its reputation before the needs of one of its pupils. Michael is a bright young man with a wicked sense of humor, and he found his own way of making a point, when he created a website called – all too appropriately – www.jksnfkdme.com. The site was online until his mother deemed it an exercise in poor judgment and made him shut it down, but only a hard-hearted soul would not laugh and sympathize.

It is clear to anyone with an interest that the education system has embraced inflexibility, and shows no sign of having any intention of helping students with special needs. Without extra help, many of these teens will develop alcohol and drug addictions, will drop out of school and become parents long before they are ready to do so, and will end up costing the state billions of dollars in welfare and Medicaid payments. Many will make their own lives miserable, and may even harm the people whom they love the most, through carelessness or a failure to control destructive emotions. We need to learn *now* that all members of society, including those who seem most problematic, deserve and need our support and help. "Problematic" groups, such as that composed of serial drug offenders serving sentence after sentence, already contain disproportionately high numbers of people with ADHD. Without treatment, understanding and special provision, we are on course for generating an entire underclass made up of people with this and other developmental disorders.

While many of the educational strategies used in elementary school, and discussed earlier in this book, are also valid for teens, some changes need to be made to reflect the young person's greater level of maturity (even if he is still lagging behind his peers) and increased need for respect as an autonomous individual. It is appropriate to start expecting him to acquire higher levels of responsibility. Tools that can help include the provision of an extra set of books at home, assistance with writing down and remembering homework duties and frequent – perhaps daily – feedback as to how he is doing. Some students will benefit from extra tuition outside school hours. To make things easier at home, parents can consider lenience about issues such as playing music while doing homework (background noise often helps ADHD people to filter out distractions) and help with creating and maintaining structure. We should never excuse antisocial behavior such as aggression, stealing or outright refusal to follow rules on the grounds that the young person has ADHD. Once again, ADHD is often an explanation for why an individual finds it hard to "follow the rules". It is never an excuse for unacceptable behavior. Educators and parents should do all they can to make it easier for the ADHD teen to follow the rules of school and home, but should not accept every deviation from acceptable behavioral standards. As is the case with small children, adolescents learn much more from their elders by observing the way in which they behave than by being given instructions.

A majority of adolescents with ADHD never make it to college or to any type of higher education. They do not make the grades, they assume that further education will be like high school and shudder at the thought of prolonging their misery. Even if they do go to college, they are often not sufficiently mature at the age of eighteen or so to deal with the challenges of living away from home and having to be responsible for managing their own time. Many are more than bright enough to embark on a degree course, but delaying this until they have become more mature has its own problems. Most people who do not enter further education within the first year of leaving high school never do. How can we ensure that our ADHD adolescents get the education they need to survive? Attending a local community college for a few years after high school can be one way to help (don't forget that it is often possible to transfer from community college to a university), and so can picking a college that is more suited to the needs of the ADHD individual; one with small classes, a smaller overall student population, and a more intimate environment. Of course, further education is not for everybody, and many people proceed to have successful lives and careers without a college education, but everyone with the intellectual ability to follow a college or university course should have the opportunity to decide whether or not to do so.

Although it can be hard for parents to admit, teenagers are no longer children. By the time the mid teens have been reached, most young men and women have acquired adult dimensions and adult physical characteristics. Along with the physical and psychological changes heralded by puberty comes the awakening of sexual desire, and interest in members of the opposite sex. Sexual desire is, of course, perfectly healthy and normal, but for a variety of valid reasons, our society prefers to make sure that it is contained for as long as possible. Of course, teenagers may not be children any more, but they are not adults either, and few parents welcome the thought of their young son or daughter freely engaging in sexual activity before the time is right. Before, I should say, *they* feel the time is right – an issue that can lead to considerable conflict between parents and teens.

Ordinary teens can find it all but impossible to resist the temptation of having sex. For the ADHD teenager, with a built-in tendency to act first and think later, struggling with reconciling adult sexual feelings with parental and social expectations and his or her own immaturity can be agonizingly difficult. This puts ADHD teens at high risk of engaging in early, unprotected sexual activity, with the attendant possibilities of unwanted pregnancy, sexually transmitted disease, and a level of physical and emotional engagement entirely inappropriate to their age and level of immaturity. Unfortunately, if parents are harsh and unbending on this issue, many kids will prefer to ensure that they are not found with condoms in their pockets than to risk getting into trouble and avoid potential disaster. As usual, forward planning is not the forte of the ADHD individual. It is foolish and naive for parents of ADHD teens to suppose that with appropriate moral training, their child will avoid early involvement in sex. It is even more foolish to imagine that by ignoring the topic, it will simply go away. Just think how many normal teenagers "can't help themselves" and get "carried away". Regardless of how strict a moral standing parents have, ADHD teens should always, *always* have access to condoms. As things stand, a huge proportion of ADHD teens are also parents, a majority of babies given up for adoption are later diagnosed as having ADHD, inherited from their biological parents, and far too many grandparents end up bringing up the baby because their ADHD teenager is just too immature to be an effective parent. In the excitement of the moment, teen parents with ADHD often insist that they love their babies and want to take care of them. Of course they do. But they are no more ready and able to be parents than a three year old is to be a responsible pet owner. The ADHD teens I meet in my office act as if the impending baby were a puppy with the same level of responsibility that a puppy requires.

Our society is an extremely sexualized one. Everyday, everywhere, teens are exposed to sexual imagery in advertising, in the movies, in literature and in music. I am not suggesting a crusade to change society – let's be realistic, popular interest in sex is not about to disappear – but the clearheadedness to understand that hormone-laden teens with a built-in inability to think before acting, are just not going to be able to say "no" to sex. As children, they always jumped first and thought about the consequences later, and they are going to go on doing the same thing now. If it feels good and it is fun, they will do it. Now, of course, the consequences are much more serious, even though ADHD teens consider them no more than they did the temptations of their childhood. Sex feels good and it is fun. Few ADHD teens will be able to resist for long.

Gay teens with ADHD do not have to worry about pregnancy, but they are at the same risk for engaging in thoughtless, reckless sex and are at elevated risk for contracting a dangerous sexually transmitted disease – especially AIDS. Again, even if parents have a strong moral stance against homosexuality and homosexual behavior, commonsense should prevail. If your teen is going to engage in potentially dangerous acts, make sure above all that he is protected, whatever your personal views may be. Preserving life and health has to come first.

The impulsivity that is an integral part of ADHD can compel teenagers towards behavior that is self-destructive and dangerous, and this includes the abuse of drugs and alcohol – something which is already an occupational hazard for all teens. To help ADHD teenagers stay away from self-destructive practices, much more intervention is needed than in the case of a normal teen. Ordinary restrictions and motivations just will not work. Remember, too, that drug-taking and alcohol abuse are usually firmly linked to a lack of self-esteem. Ultimately, an attraction to drugs will always exist among ADHD teens, for so long as they suffer from feelings of inadequacy, unhappiness and self-doubt. To treat or prevent drug use, we have to first deal with its root causes. My approach to the teenage drug users I see on a professional basis is to say, "By all means, get high (they're going to do it anyway, so I try not to seem like every other adult they encounter). But before you do, make sure that you have a good relationship with your family, that you are achieving good results in school and that you are not in any conflictful situations. Once you have accomplished all of that, get high all you want, with my blessing." The catch-22, of course, is that teenagers literally *cannot* get high and still maintain a good relationship with family, school and friends. This is my advice to teens who are using drugs because I know that it makes sense. By the time a person with ADHD reaches their teenage years, they have had authority figures telling them what to do all their lives. If I, their treating psychologist, join the ranks of the other adults in their lives, I will quickly be rejected as another mere fool who only knows about rules and punishments and remembers nothing about being young. Let's be very clear on this point, I do not ever think doing drugs is ok for anyone. Since the fact that adolescents (and most other people, too) cannot manage their lives with any degree of proficiency while using drugs, I move the focus of my advice away from the substances themselves, and towards the patient's responsibilities and relationships. When the teen is helped to recognize that major life events like achieving good grades, maintaining family relationships and keeping on top of responsibilities are not improving because of drug use, it is easier for him to decide to stop taking drugs by himself. Of course, it is never as simple as it sounds, but it does help for me to shed an authoritarian image as quickly as possible, and become viewed almost as a peer who can be trusted, or at least as an adult who has not forgotten what it feels like to be young. When a teenager comes to rely upon me firstly as a human being, they become able to provide me with a genuine picture of their life, their world and their problems. I access the child or adolescent within myself in order to help to eradicate drugs from their experience. In this, having ADHD helps to make me a better treatment provider. I know that there are ways in which I have never grown up, and that in certain aspects of my life I am still immature. It may be unorthodox, but my ADHD persona has given rise to a very effective method of treatment!

10
A New Recruit

After getting arrested for possession of eighteen ounces of pot and speed with intent to distribute, I decided that the navy would be the place for me. My friend Jimmy – he who had advised me to try the smoke detector plant – had joined, and he was very enthusiastic. Besides, telling the legal authorities that I wanted to join the navy had the effect of mitigating my sentence.

"I'm sorry," I told the boys in authority, "for having made a foolish mistake. But I want to go and serve my country, and make a good life for myself." The judge looked favorably on that, and I got off lightly, with a symbolic slap on the hand (6 months probation), in order to facilitate joining the military.

As I left the courtroom with Mom, one of the policemen walked up behind us and muttered, "Nice pot, hippy boy." We had gone down for eighteen ounces, but the boys in blue had found twenty two. More than anything, I wanted to respond angrily, but Mom shook her head at me – ("*we don't need any more trouble*") – and I knew that she was right.

So on January fourth, 1973, off I went to the Great Lakes Naval Training Center in the Windy City, Chicago. My parents had been pleased to hear that I got my high school equivalency certificate (GED), but seemed ambivalent about the news that I was going to join the navy. It was not easy to take any of my proclamations seriously – they had seen me start and not finish too many things too many times. But as usual, I did not stop and think about whether this was something I really wanted to do. I had an idea, and I acted on it, immediately: "Join the navy? Cool! Where do I sign?" Already, I had seen myself in uniform, looking smart and wowing the girls before heading off to exotic overseas locations. My friend Bear, already a navy boy, gave me some useful advice.

"When you get there," he said. "They will give you a form to fill out. To the question about whether you know how to fill out a watch bill, say 'yes'. It doesn't matter whether you really can or not, because they are going to teach you how to do it their way anyway." I also had to sign a piece of paper detailing the drugs I had taken in my life before they would let me swear in. Because I had been arrested and charged, I had to admit to having taken all the drugs on the very long list included on the recruitment form, which seemed to have been designed to identify and "weed out" the drug users. This admission was to be significant later on.

As soon as I arrived at boot camp, I knew that I had made a big mistake. If you are in the military, you get yelled at – all the time. There were few things I liked less than having someone screaming in my face. I had had more than enough of that at high school. For the moment, however, I could not do very much about it.

Because I had said that I knew how to fill in a watch bill as my friend Bear had advised, I was assigned to be first platoon leader, making me an instant authority figure to the other new recruits who had not shared my inside information. I coped for a while. Military society is so highly structured that people with ADHD just do not have time to allow the disability to express itself. There is not a moment when you are not told what you have to do, and where you have to be. Spontaneity has very little leeway for expression.

After a month or so of getting by, I was walking through the camp one day when I heard somebody call my name.

"What the hell?" I wondered. "Nobody ever calls my name in here." I looked around, and saw my friend Bear. He walked over to me gave me a very welcome hug, and handed me a couple of joints, already rolled, with the warning to be careful. Now, that was too much temptation for me. At the time I was on a thing called "service week." As the first platoon leader of my company, my service week task was to take a brand new company of recruits and initiate them into the first military experience they had had. Simply put, my job was to leave my company for a week and get a new company situated with their new haircuts, uniforms and general military necessities. This was a perfect job for me since it left me almost entirely unsupervised and with a little authority to boot. The night I received the pot from Bear, I got out of bed, locked myself in the bathroom closet and lit up. If you are in the navy and you get caught doing even soft drugs, you get serious jail time. I knew that, but did I think about it? No way. I just thought about getting high. My ADHD kicked in and made the decision for me. I wanted to get high, and I wanted to do it right there and then, not at some more apt point in the future – as if there would be a more apt point.

In the morning, some of the boys in my company told me that they knew what I had been doing. They had heard me getting into the closet, and recognized the distinctive smell when I lit up. I denied it, of course, but they were not fools and several of them looked as though they had it in mind to turn me in, perhaps thinking that they would earn some bonus points that way. I threw away the second joint out of pure fear!

It was very clear that the navy was not for me. I had been suggested for training in a specialized field and had achieved the highest score any recruit had ever made in the aptitude test, but I just could not take another day of being screamed at and of being the property of Uncle Sam, whether I wanted to be or not. How could I get out? I knew that when you sign a contract with the military, they own you, body and soul, and they do not let you go without a fight, but I had an idea.

First, I went to see the doctor, and claimed – falsely – that I had been suffering from Acid flashbacks (those random moments allegedly suffered by former LSD users which simulate the original LSD high), and really needed something to calm me down.

For the first time in my life, I had a full-blown plan that went from beginning to end with all the details in the middle and this was the first step.

The first person I spoke to was an admissions officer. He heard my story, and looked at me sharply.

"Sit down against the wall," he told me. "You are now in breach of contract." He assumed that I had denied drug use on the application form about having taken drugs in the past, which, of course, I had not. I knew that I was not in breach of contract, but he did not. So far, so good. The first stage of the plan had been a success.

I did my best to look upset, but that was exactly what I had wanted to hear. If they thought I was in breach of contract, they would throw me out, and I would be free to go. When the doctor came in, he repeated that I was in breach of contract, and warned me that I was not likely to be in the navy much longer. I tried to look even more depressed, while inwardly I was excited. So far, things were going just as I wanted.

That very day, I was removed from my service week duties and sent back to my original company, where the commanding officer called me to see him. He screamed in my face that he did not want any drug addicts in his company, any free-love, free-wheeling useless hippies like me. I was sent two days later to the special indoctrination division, or SID, otherwise known as the "sorry I did it" division. It was not fun. It was January, it was Chicago, it was freezing, and my job was to clear the packed ice from the streets where the sailors marched, for fourteen hours a day. I was so relieved that the officers were out of my face that chipping ice was a welcome, albeit mindless, task to fill my empty time and I did not complain as I attended to my duties.

Before finalizing my exit from the navy, I was sent to see a psychiatrist whose job it was to see if I was really having drug induced flashbacks, or if I was making the whole thing up. I talked to him for what seemed like an eternity. He asked me endless questions but did not write anything down, and I could tell that he was unconvinced. I knew I had to hit this pompous ass with something that was going to knock his socks off in order to get him on my side. Eventually, I remembered that what I was supposed to be doing was convincing him that I was having problems with the side effects of illegal drugs, so I provided him with a lurid description of an actual Acid trip. I gave him as many details as I could remember and even made some up for dramatic effect: "I see all these colors and things moving … and then I feel as though I am part of it all, like I am one with everything. Then I start to feel like I am floating and even flying (flying hallucinations were big in the media back then and everyone was afraid that those weird hippies on drugs would think they were superman and try to fly out the window of a high rise building). And then sometimes I want to chase the colors around the room and laugh and fly with them as they soar up to the sky, if you know what I mean." I looked at him dreamily.

He picked up a pen and started to write. *Hot damn!* That had been the right thing to say! As he wrote feverishly I began to dance a jig inside. I knew that I was as good as on my way home

"May I ask what you're writing?" I inquired.

"I'm writing my opinion as to whether you should stay in my navy or not," he replied.

"And what do you think?" I asked with a look of fear and trepidation.

"I think that you should get the hell out of my navy," he barked. "We don't need drug addicts like you dragging the quality of our boys down. This is not the right place for someone like you. My navy is for men that can handle life without drugs, not weak people like you who have to rely on those hippie drugs to handle the pressure."

I did my best to look despondent, but I was rejoicing. I was going to be free! My plan was bearing fruit.

The next day, the navy lawyer summoned me to his office.

"You know," he told me, "you should not be in so much trouble. You are not in breach of contract, because you admitted to the drugs before signing up."

"I know that," I confessed.

"Well," he asked. "Do you want in or out?" I was afraid this was a loaded question, but I had to take the chance and hope that he was just doing his job and going through the motions.

"I want out."

He looked at me curiously and said, "That's fine, good luck as a civilian." The lawyer turned and left, sending me on my way towards freedom and a life filled with the twists and turns of ADHD.

Before my departure could be finalized, I had to put in some time working while waiting for my departure orders. I was assigned to clean out the swimming pool, which suited me just fine. I loved swimming, and in order to clean the pool I had to be in the water. I was cleaning one day when Dad called, promising to intervene. He pulled a few strings and congressman James Cleveland got in touch to tell me that he could sort everything out, and even get me a promotion if that is what I wanted him to do for me.

"It's all taken care of," he told me. "I'll even make sure you get whatever rank you want. There is no need for you to spend your time doing menial work."

"Thank you very much for your effort," I replied in a respectful, humble tone. "I appreciate your concern, but the discharge process is underway and I think it is better if I go through with it."

The next day, I was on my way home to Mom and Dad's house, and to my girlfriend Karen, whose family had moved from Hingham to the same New Hampshire town as mine. Officially, I was being sent home with my tail between my legs, but inside I was brimming over with satisfaction. For the first time in my life, I had put a complex plan into action, and followed it through. From start to finish, I had been in control. I had outsmarted the navy! OK, outsmarting the navy might not sound like such a big deal as all that, considering the disdain that most military boys have for the intellect. But nonetheless, this was a victory for me. I wanted out, and I got out, with an honorable discharge. They could not give me a dishonorable discharge, because I had never lied to anyone. So as far as I was concerned, this was one in the eye for everyone who had misused their authority against me, from kindergarten up. I fought the law – and *I won* (as Eric Clapton almost put it). In my own chaotic way, I had taken a decisive step towards adulthood.

11
Moving on up

> *"I know that Richard thought we wrote him off as a total loser. There is little doubt we knew he was going through a bad phase. But I don't think we wrote him off entirely."* – Bill Kuendig

In 1973, I was out of the navy, back home and working in my father's latest factory as an operator on the factory floor. My responsibility was to manage one of the automatic screw machines during the afternoon to midnight shift. The job was boring, noisy and oily but the money was not bad for a man of my age and the shift allowed me to sleep late in the mornings. I managed to stay for two or three years, hating every minute of the job, but keeping things together. It could have been worse. For the first time, I was maintaining a fairly even keel. I lived at home and had a long standing girlfriend, Karen, and essentially nothing to worry about.

As a child, I had never been able to conquer sports. As an adolescent and young adult, I finally discovered a sport that I was good at – martial arts. Bruce Lee was my hero, and for once I had found something that I could really apply myself to.

"Bruce Lee has his act together," I reasoned, "so if I am like him, I will too." So off to the dojo (gym) it was. Eventually, I earned three black belts in three separate martial arts. By then, however, my family had already categorized me as "the one who can't do sports" and no one was very interested in my achievements, although I was dying to show off. I knew that I was good, but I wanted – no, *needed* – recognition. It was my turn to shine, damn it! Couldn't anybody see that? I was too proud to say so, but one of the reasons why I had worked so hard to earn my belts had been to show my family that I was good at something, anything!

At this time, I moved into my own apartment, my relationship with Karen moved up a notch, and we decided to marry. As usual, the decision had been made with almost no thought or planning: "Let's get married! It'll be great. Who cares if we don't really have anything in common and keep arguing? Love is all that matters, right?"

Appearances suggested that some stability had entered my life, although when I looked at myself in the mirror, I did not see a young man with steady, if menial, employment, knowledge of the martial arts, and a fiancée. Even though the *process* of change had begun, I saw the same loser I had always assumed myself to be. If others saw a reasonably well-adjusted, ambitious, young man, I was clearly deluding them, and I was afraid that some day I would be caught out. I guess I thought that marriage might make it harder for people to notice that I was not all I really seemed to be. If I had a wife, I would not stand out. I would look just like everybody else, despite knowing inside that I was somehow, indefinably, different. Above all, the ring on my finger would be proof that there was at least one person who actually liked me the way I was.

I was not a very religious man, but the events of the following few months really suggest that God had other plans for me; that he did not want me spending the rest of my life operating an automatic screw machine. First of all, my apartment burned down after I fell asleep with a candle burning beside the bed on a plastic table, recalling the incident of the burning tent of some years earlier and prompting a similar reaction from me: "Holy shit! How did that happen?" But yes, I was drunk again and didn't wake up until it was far too late.

Then, about six months before the wedding date Karen told me that she did not want to marry me, and that she was going to marry my best friend instead. I was devastated, to say the least.

I had been ready to spend the rest of my life with the woman I thought I loved. Some of the wedding invitations had already been ordered and her revelation was a surprise to everyone, not just me. Her affair with my friend had been kept well hidden. Maybe someone with a finer eye for details would have noticed the many small changes in her behavior, but that just wasn't me. ADHD had done it to me again. I didn't even see that, right under my nose, my fiancé and my best friend were having an affair. One of the text book symptoms of ADHD is "fails to give close attention to details or makes careless mistakes…" and I sure did! We could never have been happy together, but I did not know that at the time, and advice like, "Some day you'll be glad it happened sooner rather than later," did not do very much to mitigate the pure emotional horror I had to endure.

Finally, I was standing at the washbasin at work one evening with a colleague, a much older man who had worked in the factory for a very long time. Even after he had washed his hands carefully, they were still lined with grease and looked just as dirty as if he had not washed them at all.

"What's going on?" I asked him. "Why are your hands still dirty even after washing them?"

He laughed. "Just wait until you've been in the business as long as me," he said. "You'll have hands as dirty as mine. After a few years, it just doesn't go away. You'll get used to it." He dried his hands on the roller-towel, said good night and left to go home.

"No way!" I thought. "I don't want to spend my life with dirty hands. I want a clean hands job." I had had a vision of myself still operating the machines twenty years later, with grimy hands, a paunch and little to show for all my hard work, and I did not like it. I left my job early, went home and told Dad that I had quit. Not just because I was bored, or tired of operating the oily machines, but because I wanted to go to college. I, Dick the perennial failure, had had enough.

My father did not believe a word of it. Not for an instant!

When I arrived at home before my work shift had finished, Dad was furious. Remember that he was also the company CEO. It was already shameful enough having a son doing menial work in his factory, let alone a son who could not even do that! Like most fathers, Dad was ambitious for his sons. He wanted us to succeed and he had his own firm notions of what success entailed. I had flunked out of school but, he considered, perhaps with the right encouragement, I would be able to work my way up through the ranks of the blue-collar employees at his firm.

"There's no way that you can get into a college," he screamed in rage. "You have done nothing but flunk everything in your life. And the only things you didn't flunk, you quit (remember that another text book ADHD symptom is "fails to finish school, work, chores or duties…")! What self-respecting college would want a loser like you? What makes you think that you will finish college when you have never finished anything before? There is just no way that is going to happen! Do you honestly believe that all your teachers were wrong about you all these years? Have you lost all grip on reality? You have about as much chance of getting into college as a snowball has in Hell!"

Dad's tirade, which I had experienced millions of times before, seemed to last forever. He was right, and we both knew it. It was true that I had either failed out of or quit almost everything that I had started. Beginning ambitious projects was easy, but finishing them was painfully difficult, as it often still is. In high school, many days had begun well, but ended by my leaving early. My grade point average would have reduced any self-respecting university acceptance committee to helpless laughter ("Who does this joker think he is? We'd never let someone like this into our university").

Despite everything, I was determined, and eventually Dad came around and came through for me as he had so many times before, because although he was frustrated with me, he never really stopped hoping for me and trying to help me in any way he could. His jeers and doubts did not cease, but he did tell me to call and ask for an application form for as many schools as I could think of. That is exactly what I did. I applied to every school I thought I had a chance of getting into, even though I was unsure of my likelihood of success. I expected to have to talk my way into higher education.

Rejection letter after rejection letter arrived, and I began to become discouraged. When my final application was refused, I decided that I had nothing to lose, and on the my father's encouragement called the president of a small college about an hour away from where I lived in New Hampshire. After three or four phone calls, I was rewarded with an appointment to meet the president of Franklin Pierce College (FPC). I still owe a great debt of thanks to Mr. Walter Peterson who, at the time, was the president of FPC for having faith in a young man with a dubious record and nothing but his ambition to recommend him.

I can remember the moment I entered his office as if it were yesterday. I looked confident, but I was as scared as could be. Remember that I had never managed to have a healthy relationship with anyone in authority – and now I wanted someone in authority to look kindly on me. To be honest, although I had learned how to speak respectfully to my "superiors" I was not inclined to do so largely because so few had given me any reason to feel respect – and I was not quite sure how to put my past behind me for a brief time. As Dr. Barkley so aptly said, ADHD is not a disorder of *knowing* what to do, but of *doing* what you know. I knew how to schmooz and kiss ass, but actually doing it was a chore I had not been called upon to do very often before.

Mr. Peterson was a large man with a formidable handshake, but a genuine and caring smile, and I started to feel more at ease as I summarized my life to date, finishing my plea with the words, "Please, Mr. Peterson, if you accept me into the college *I will not fail*." This was the first time that I had said those words in earnest, not just as a manipulative technique, and it felt strange to mean them, and to feel that, despite everything, I would be able to deal with the challenges I was presenting myself with.

Mr. Peterson asked me to come back after the lunch break, to allow him time to discuss my case with his registrar. On my return, he presented me with a stoic appearance and some good news; I had been accepted into Franklin Pierce College, with one very strict condition. Under no circumstance was I to get any grade less than a C. I would be out on my ear with the first low grade I received. The tension dropped from my shoulders. I was in! Wow. Somehow, I'd managed to convince Mr. Peterson that I was OK. I wondered how long it would take him to find out that I was a bad person, but quickly repressed that thought and focused on the future. Perhaps now, after all these years, I had found a way to make Mom and Dad proud, and secure a clean-hands job for myself in the process. Perhaps now I would stop being the failure of the family, lagging behind my bright, successful siblings. Perhaps now, people would start to think that I was OK, after all.

Going to college at the age of twenty-two marked the end of my adolescence. In tacit recognition of this, I told everyone that I did not want to be called "Dick" any more. From now on, my name was going to be "Richard". I was a man, and I wanted a man's name, not that of a little boy. I was going to a place where no-one knew me, where I could start again. It was a new lease on life. Retrospectively, I can identify this moment as the beginning of a new level of insight into myself. At the time, I often used the phrase: "Dickie is dead. Richard is alive." On some level, I had decided to take charge of the

ADHD I did not know I had, instead of letting it remain in charge of me. It really was a kind of rebirth; born-again Christians often refer to themselves as having two birth dates – their biological ones, and the ones that mark the anniversary of the day that they started to live according to a new ethos and understanding. In a secular context, starting college was not at all unlike that for me.

College life was wonderful. As a man of twenty-two with ADHD, my level of maturity was equivalent to that of a normal seventeen or eighteen year old – just the right age to leave home and acquire new interests and responsibilities. I was like a kid in a candy shop. The college I attended was relatively small – about 1,500 students – with a friendly, intimate campus full, and I mean *full*, of beautiful young women, all of whom were just as eager for new experiences as I was. These were the early 1970s and we were reaping the benefits of the sexual revolution of the previous decade. Young people were not just allowed to have sex and fun, they were *supposed* to. It was practically a duty and I was so very dutiful! I had been a navy boy, had I not? I knew about fulfilling one's duties, and I sure did fulfill them. It had hurt when Karen left me, but now the dividends were coming in and I was more than happy to be young, free and single. There was a party every night, and life was good. I had a great roommate, Paul, whom I still love to this day, and we quickly became inseparable, united by empathy, mutual interests, and an unceasing quest for enjoyment. For us, the good life meant fun and girls. And booze and drugs. Of course.

I was finally on the right track and for the last time I almost threw it away, when I earned abysmal grades for the first semester. I had taken four classes – College Math, English One, Anthropology and Spanish. I coped adequately, if not well, with the first three, but Spanish was a total bust! Put in hours of my valuable time to learn the grammar and vocabulary of a language I did not think I would ever use? It hardly seemed worth the effort, and I was given a well-deserved F. I had been busy, but I certainly had not been studying. Shortly after my grades came out, I was called to the president's office. I pleaded with Mr. Peterson to let me stay, despite our initial agreement.

"My circumstances are special ones," I pleaded. "I have been out of school for five years, so it is harder for me to get back into the system. Cs in three out of four subjects really isn't that bad considering everything."

Mr. Peterson was unconvinced. He spoke of the college's need to maintain standards, and the fact that I had only made it in thanks to his good will.

This is what I looked like in college. You can see from my eyes that I still enjoyed getting stoned!

"I can't leave," I thought to myself. "Being here is like being in Heaven." I was horrified to find myself on the verge of tears. How unmanly!

"Well, Richard," he responded. "If you want to stay in Heaven, you'll just have to start paying your dues. Everyone deserves a chance, and you have already had yours." But he relented, and extended my probation.

From then on, I divided my time between my passion for fun and a new passion; the study of psychology. Initially, I had planned to study anthropology, but I was deeply impressed by one of my psychology professors – Professor Jack, as we knew him. Professor Jack was my new hero. He understood *everything*, and was completely unlike any hero I had ever had before. Rather than being a lean, mean martial arts expert or a wild joker, he was the archetypal absent-minded, but brilliant professor, with the tweed jacket and abstracted air that accompany the role.

One day, I was looking idly from my dorm window on the fourth floor when I saw Professor Jack cross the campus and – walk headfirst into a tree! I laughed so hard that I literally fell off my chair. The next day when I went into class, Professor Jack looked at me sternly, and said, "I heard you laughing at me yesterday."

"I'm sorry," I said, starting to laugh again. "But I have never seen anything so funny in my life. How can anyone walk into a tree? It was right in front of you!"

He looked surprised that I should have to ask such a question, and answered simply, "I was thinking."

Thinking! He could not have said anything more profound. I had never conceived of a person who could be so lost in thought as to become oblivious of his surroundings. *Professor Jack had been thinking so hard that he walked into a tree!* And now I wanted to be like that, too. I wanted to walk into trees, if that was what it was going to take to be the sort of person that others respected. I wanted to learn how it felt to be absorbed by thought.

Four years after starting college, I graduated cum laude with honors in Psychology. I had had to fight against my problems with sitting down long enough to read, struggling with the temptation to party instead of study, and controlling my tendency to take so many drugs that I just was not able to study at all. I had had to learn how to spend at least four hours in the university library, seven days a week. And I had managed it all. From the day that Mr. Peterson gave me "one last chance" until the very last day of school, my grades never dropped below a B, for the simple reason that I knew my priorities; parties and girls. This may seem trite and superficial now, but the truth is that these were the lures that kept me going and prompted me to strive for academic excellence. In practice today, I often help the ADHD child, adolescent or adult develop priorities on which to build success by pointing out the tangible benefits of prolonged effort, rather than suggesting that hard work is its own reward. Hard work *is not* its own reward! In my case, I knew that I wanted to party and to be surrounded by attractive, young female undergraduates. I also knew that in order to keep these two things in my life, I had to earn the grades necessary to stay in the hallowed ground of the college. A simple cost-benefit analysis was easy. Poor grades would mean losing out on what I wanted most, right now. Thoughts of a career or long-term gains were irrelevant. Poor grades simply meant losing access to girls and parties, and good grades meant I could keep on having fun. It was an easy choice to make, and the education I obtained along the way was simply a beneficial side effect. In psychology, there is a thing called the "Premack Principle" which states that if you put off the desired activity (going to parties) until the undesired activity (studying) is complete, you will increase the occurrence of the undesired activity (positive reinforcement). I was using the Premack Principle without even knowing it and it was really working!

Doing well in college was the first big success of my entire life, but even on my graduation day, it was hard for those who knew me well to stop thinking of me as a habitual loser. My brother John came to my graduation, and he still remembers the tangibility of my satisfaction with having achieved so ordinary an accomplishment ("It was one of the first times I saw how proud you were ... you strutted around the campus and ceremony like a little kid"). I had not yet quite earned the parental approval I strove for, however. My graduation gift from Mom and Dad? A pen. After all the work I had done? After having to change from high-school dropout to successful college graduate? That really hurt! I guess that they were still hurting and angry, on some level, about the misery I'd put them through throughout my childhood and adolescence. But overall, our relationship was getting better, and acquiring adult dimensions. Although I still had undiagnosed ADHD, I seemed to be happier, more respectful and able to cope with the demands of society. I had learned how to play the game, if not completely, then to a reasonable extent. Mom and Dad no longer had to feel apologetic about their youngest son and I knew that I was beginning to repay them for the fact that, despite everything, they had never quite given up on me.

I graduated from FPC when I was twenty-six, with a Bachelors degree. What to do with my new qualifications? I enrolled in another college in Akron, Ohio, to study for a masters degree, and my roommate Paul came to stay with me. I made ends meet by working as a dorm caretaker, for which I received a free apartment and, as my best friend, Paul came along for the ride. I studied, but Paul and I also continued to party hard. Alcohol and drugs still played an important part in my life, but as my responsibilities grew, my drug-taking decreased and, little by little, getting high ceased to be one of my priorities. I graduated from Akron, Paul married his fiancée Pam and I moved to California to start studying for my doctoral degree. Paul wasn't far behind.

Did the growing list of qualifications under my belt make me feel better about myself? Well, even when I got my doctorate in psychology, I was not able to shake off the idea that I was inherently unworthy. Before, every time I achieved something, I felt that I was deceiving the examination board and my friends and family. Now, with a doctorate, I felt like an even bigger charlatan. Instead of deceiving those around me, I was deceiving the world. *Doctor* Kuendig? Who did I think I was kidding? I may have seemed cocky and sure of myself on the outside, but chaos still courted me at every turn and the frightened little boy I had been remained with me. That little boy has never really gone away. Years of being told that they are stupid and will never amount to anything leaves ADHD people with scars that just do not disappear.

12
Making the Trip to Adulthood

As I mention above, most ADHD teens remain adolescents, psychologically speaking, until they are well into their twenties. This can make it difficult to make a successful transition to college or to the workplace, as individuals with ADHD often lack the maturity to make important decisions, and to be responsible for their own time. They still need extra support and help from their parents, instructors and peers. But, as I have also said before, ADHD is not an excuse for destroying your life. It is a major contributing factor to many ruined lives, but *it does not have to be*. It is possible to grow up, despite having ADHD (even if one's inner child remains more prominent than is the case with most people). Above all, with the right help, there is no reason in the world why people with ADHD cannot become successful, fulfilled adults with flourishing careers and stable relationships.

It was not until relatively recently that ADHD was recognized as a condition that persists into adulthood and, quite rightly, patients who present with ADHD-like symptoms have to be carefully investigated before being diagnosed as having the condition. An adult individual is not considered to have ADHD unless it can be shown that he manifested the symptoms of the condition for a minimum of six months prior to the age of seven, and not until other causes – both organic and psychological – have been ruled out as causing his symptoms.

How can adults and emerging adults with ADHD maximize their chances of succeeding in life? First of all, families and friends need to allow the individual with ADHD some extra time to mature. Even if he has made good grades in high school and is able to start college or embark on a career, he may have some trouble with schedules, time-keeping and order, as well experiencing as some delays in reaching emotional maturity.

This is where parents and/or partners can help a lot – not by organizing everything for him, but by helping him to organize himself. A young man I treated was bright, intelligent and ambitious, but he kept losing one job after another because he just never managed to get into work on time and, one by one, his employers lost patience with their unreliable employee. Together, we worked out some strategies to help – a shaving kit he kept in the car so that, if necessary, he could groom himself at work; a second set of clean clothes at the office, and a back-up alarm clock to make sure that he woke on time. His partner agreed to help him to make sure that the coping mechanisms were always in place. Expensive? No. Complicated? Not at all. Yet these straightforward approaches to his problems with getting organized and staying that way made a big difference just as practical approaches to homework help the child earlier in life. It is often as simple as that.

Of course, the best way to ensure that the ADHD adult will be able to achieve professional and personal success in life is to provide him with the appropriate care and treatment long before adulthood is reached. Diagnosis and treatment in childhood help the individual with a behavioral disability to grow up healthfully, and with the means with which to compensate for weaknesses and build upon strengths, as well as increasing the likelihood that adolescence will be survived without the problems of drug and alcohol abuse, reckless driving and sexual behavior and general unruliness that so often beset ADHD teens. However, it is *never* too late to start working towards a better future life. Of course it is harder to change one's ingrained behavioral patterns in adulthood, but the dividends (more success at work, happier marriages and more able parenting, to name just a few) make the effort more than worthwhile.

As you know, many young people with ADHD do not make it to college, in many cases because of the lack of support they have been given by their elementary and high school teachers and their associated failure to acquire the necessary level of control over their powers of retention, concentration and effort applied over time. However, to look at this difficult issue positively, it can be said that, with the right help and support, there is no reason why individuals with ADHD should not attend a college or university and indeed the privilege of spending a few more years in education instead of being thrust headlong into the workforce allows the individual more time to mature, as well as developing his intellect and work skills. People with ADHD are just as likely to be bright as anybody else, and many will be surprised to find that higher education is, in many ways, a lot more interesting and manageable than school ever was. They will be choosing the subjects that interest them to study, and that makes a huge difference. Many people with ADHD can sustain effort over time when the task at hand is not tedious for them and studying a topic that flames your interests is very different to the rote learning of some boring subject that just happens to be on the national curriculum. At college, there are usually ample opportunities for students to move around between lectures, unlike school where students can be expected to sit still for hours on end. No less important is the fact that university students are not subject to the humiliation of being treated as children, without legitimate desires and ambitions, as young men and women of seventeen and eighteen routinely are in high school.

Not everyone realizes that the legal provision that should guarantee a decent education for ADHD students at elementary and high school level should also apply to university students (remember that the Individuals with Disabilities Education Act makes provision for "children" up to the age of 21). They will have to work as hard as or harder than everybody else, but some accommodations can be made to minimize the effects of their disability, such as the provision of extra time during tests, or of a quiet spot without distractions in which to sit them. It is incumbent upon the individual in question to alert the school authorities to the fact that they have a disability, and to ask for reasonable provisions to be made. Flunking an examination and only then asking for special consideration on the grounds of having a developmental disability is not acceptable, nor should it be. When the ADHD student has told the authorities that he needs some extra help at times, and has been given that extra help, the ball is in his court and he will, quite simply, have to study, possibly putting in more hours than other students without a developmental disorder. I did not receive extra help in getting into college or in making it through my first semester, but by that time I knew that there was only one person who could ensure that I would graduate; me. Believe me, however, accommodations for my ADHD would have made the long educational journey I went through much more manageable.

University degrees are supposed to be measures of excellence, and they will lose their value for everybody if they are simply handed out in return for putting in a cursory appearance. ADHD should never be used as an excuse for deliberate shoddiness, or for the conscious decision to spend time slacking instead of studying. Equal rights for people with disabilities is about making sure that the playing ground is as even as it can possibly be, not giving a free ride to those who happen to have extra hurdles to jump. And when the student with ADHD graduates successfully in the field of his choice, he knows that his achievements have been won with even greater effort than those of his non-ADHD peers. He has not allowed his disability to become a handicap!

Whether or not the person with ADHD goes to college, he will need to make that all-important decision; what am I going to do? This is a decision that we all have to make, but arriving at the right answer can be much more difficult for the person with ADHD than for others, especially as the decision may have to be made when the individual is still, for all intents and purposes, an adolescent. For example, just before sitting down to write this chapter, I was talking with an 18 year old man with ADHD who said that he believed that his time in high school afforded him the right to take a month off from everything! His father and step mother did not agree with his decision to put off getting a job at all, but did allow him the latitude to make that kind of a decision. Now that he is a high school graduate without work, however, they also decided that they would no longer support him financially.

There are many factors that bear upon the ADHD adult's likelihood of success in the world of work. Many people with ADHD spend their lives wandering from one low-income job to another, and even drift in and out of crime because, as their impulsive side sees it, it offers large rewards without having to go to major effort. Too often, they do not look at the real outcome of involvement in crime; a life spent behind bars. It does not have to be that way. Not surprisingly, the people behind the statistics demonstrate that a huge proportion of criminals and other problematic people with ADHD were never treated, or never treated satisfactorily, to compensate for the disability and many ultimately ended up in the legal system.

With proper treatment and care throughout childhood and adolescence, there is no reason at all why the individual with ADHD cannot succeed in building a successful career. That said, not all careers are necessarily the best choices for the person with ADHD. To maximize the chances of professional success, some careful planning has to be done. What are the principle symptoms of the condition? Difficulty with maintaining attention and effort over time, problems with self-organization and discipline. Right. So working as an accountant, an archivist or on an assembly line is probably out of the question and this should be borne in mind when deciding what to study at the university, or what career to enter as an apprentice on leaving high school. Plenty of adults with ADHD do not succeed in their chosen careers because they have chosen the *wrong* career, not because they could not succeed if they had made a wiser choice. Remember that most of us spend a huge proportion of our waking hours engaged in working. To make these hours as happy and fulfilling as possible, it is important to carefully study our strengths and weaknesses so as to understand what career suits our aptitudes and personality best. Before deciding what to do, the ADHD individual needs to work through a series of steps, starting by asking a series of important questions:

What strengths can I bring to the workplace? People with ADHD are often very innovative and energetic. These can be positive attributes to bring to many careers, especially those which require one to make snap decisions and be spontaneous. When and how do spontaneity and impulsivity enhance, rather than damage, career performance?

What are my weaknesses? If you have ADHD, chances are that these will entail getting into work on time, getting projects finished for deadlines, concentrating during long, tedious meetings, and the like. Clearly, some careers involve more boring meetings, strict deadlines and killer punctuality than others.

Do I really want to do what seems like such a good idea to me at the moment, or is it just a reckless impulse? It is not a good idea to make important decisions hastily. I thought I wanted to be in the navy – until a couple of days after I signed the contract. Then, I wanted out. If you think that lion-taming might be fun, it may be that you will have to try it and get a limb bitten off in order to determine that that career is not for you. I am sorry, but those unfortunate few with ADHD almost always need to experience the consequence of their impulses before abandoning them!

A girl or boy with ADHD is going to grow up to be first an adolescent and then a woman or man with ADHD, period. Countless examples have shown this to be true, and there is no point in fighting it. This is not, however, advice to be defeatist, just realistic. Understanding that people with ADHD will probably take longer to become mature (about 30% longer) is important, as is realizing that the ADHD is going to have to continue to be managed. Transition from adolescence to adulthood is rarely completely smooth, but it can be done, and it can be done successfully.

13
All Grown up with ADHD

On completing my doctorate, I left California and moved to Omaha, Nebraska where I was going to head up an adolescent psychiatric unit at a local hospital. My time there was quite unremarkable except for one throw back to my past, involving my supervisor. He was a wonderful man named Duane, a psychologist who made no bones of letting his close associates know he was gay. Duane immediately impressed me as one of those men who have a gentle nature and a genuine empathy for their fellow humans. At that time, I was teaching a combination undergraduate/graduate class at Creighton University in adolescent psychology and the beginning of my career was looking pretty good. Then, one fateful night I was shopping at the local grocery store when my pager went off, signaling me to call Duane. I panicked instantly! Because of the unusual time, I knew that I must be in trouble because of some im-

My wedding day. Typically, I'm the only one not paying attention to what is going on!

pulsive mistake I had made. I paced around the grocery store mentally listing that I was required to do, but I could not figure out what my defense was going to be because I could not determine what I had screwed up. Years of living with ADHD had left me with the belief that I was only ever summoned when I had done something very wrong. Now, I was sure, I was in line for a reprimand. I knew I couldn't put off calling Duane much longer. He was my boss and when he called I was obligated to call him back, even though I did not want to. As my blood pressure rose and my anxiety level started to become unmanageable, I called Duane. I was fully convinced that I had done something so terrible that I was going to be terminated there and then. Duane answered his phone.

"Hi Duane, this is Richard, what's up?" I said, trying to sound relaxed. There was a pause that seemed to last an eternity, although it cannot have been more than a couple of seconds.

"Oh yes, Richard," Duane replied. "Would you like to go out to dinner tonight?" All my paranoia had been for naught. I had reacted to this gentle man as if he had been a reprimand waiting to happen. My reaction was not to my current circumstances but to the years of training I had undergone at the hands of ADHD. Because, over the years, I had learned that interactions with authority figures always meant that I was in trouble, it seemed logical that this interaction was going to be unpleasant and defensive, just like all the others. But it was not. I had reacted in a way that was inappropriate to my current situation. My past was over and those days of foolish, impulsive and child-like behaviors were now a curse I had to divorce myself from so that I could begin to move on into adulthood.

I stayed in Omaha for about a year and then moved back to Ohio because my father was in poor health and I was the only sibling who was somewhat mobile at that point. My lifelong friend Paul had settled down in the area with his wife. I was excited to put my training into practice, and pleased to know that my best friend would be nearby as we both set about the business of being professional adults.

Paul visited on countless occasions to help me fix up my property – putting in a fence and digging drainage trenches. I appreciated his efforts, but it never occurred to me that he was expecting concrete returns for his actions. I had not called around to his house to help him paint and hammer and saw. If had asked me to help, I would not have hesitated for a moment. Paul was my best friend, and we had spent those crucial years of early adulthood in each other's company. There was nothing I would not have done for him. But I never realized that I should be helping him out right now, with the chores involved in making his house a home. Without being told what he expected, I simply did not know what I was supposed to do, nor did I entertain the idea that he had certain expectations of me. Those unwritten laws of society can really be too subtle at times! Being friends with a person with ADHD requires some extra understanding. Failing to pick up and interpret subtle cues about behavioral expectations is typical of the adult with ADHD, who can remain oblivious with the best will in the world. Eventually, Paul grew tired of always being the one who remembered to be thoughtful and began to think that I was not reciprocating because I did not care about him. Our friendship faltered, and remains "on hold". I wish I could go back and put things right, because after literally living together for nearly 10 years the friendship is gone and I still can only guess why that is. Paul will not talk to me any more. A mutual friend did throw away a remark, saying that I considered myself "too good for him." Nothing could be further from the truth.

If Paul had communicated to me what his expectations were, I would have eagerly met them. But at the time of writing, our friendship has fallen victim to the scourge of ADHD and the perceived insensitivity it engenders.

I have few friends left from my past. One by one, they have left my life, and I attribute this in large part to the fact that I have the disability that I do, ADHD. Blurting out remarks without thinking, failing to understand others' needs without being explicitly informed about them, being unable to second-guess concerns – all of this is part of the reality of being an adult with ADHD, and I know that these lacks are a serious barrier to ongoing friendship and closeness. I deeply regret these deficiencies in myself, and sadly recognize that they are an integral part of the condition I suffer from and continually try to overcome.

Friendship with an adult ADHD sufferer requires more patience than ordinary friendship. If I could do anything to stop having the condition, I would. But I cannot, so I am just going to have to accept a reduced social circle. I have a good life. I have my wonderful wife, a few wonderfully close friends, a house full of gadgets and toys, and a whole lot to be thankful for. As a university graduate with ADHD, I am a member of a tiny minority. Few people with the disability are fortunate enough to make it to university, and the day does not pass when I do not count my blessings.

Let me rewind for a moment. I have my wonderful wife. In this, too, I am particularly blessed. Adults with ADHD are especially prone to marital discord and divorce. Somehow, I have managed to escape. How did I manage that? That is a question I often ask myself when I look at Miran and realize how happy I am; a thousand times happier than I thought I would ever be.

I met my wife Miran shortly after she moved to the United States from her native Korea. I was studying for my doctorate at that time, and she was combining learning English with her career as a contemporary dancer. I was smitten immediately (thank *God* I did not marry Karen, all those years before…) and we started a relationship. For practical reasons, the first five years of our partnership were spent mostly apart, and we maintained our closeness by writing and meeting whenever it was possible (see how maintaining effort over time is possible for the person with ADHD when the rewards are tangible?). At this time, I had still not been diagnosed as having ADHD, but Miran accepted my recklessness and impulsivity as part of who I am, and never tried to change me. She raised her eyebrows when she saw me exchange one shiny new car for another time after time, just for the fun of driving a new vehicle. But, "That's just Richard!" she reasoned.

Eventually, we were able to stay in the same place at the same time, and we were married. This time, there was no doubt that I had done the right thing. Mom and Dad both loved Miran as soon as they met her, and our wedding was wonderful, even when my brother John took it upon himself to play a tape of my love messages to Miran to the assembled guests!

After the celebrations were over, I cried. The emotion behind the tears was a strange mixture of joy and sorrow. I had married the love of my life, and I was also saying goodbye to a turbulent and often troubled past. The impulsivity that can be such a difficult aspect of having ADHD can be a blessing at times. I know that many American males work hard at repressing their feelings, and lose out as a result. I am not ashamed of the strength of my feelings, and I do let tears fall when they come. Am I less of a man for that? I don't think so. At the time of my marriage, I recognized that I had taken an important step away from the chaos of my earlier life, but that chaos still did not have a name.

The realization that the problems I had struggled with all my life were due to ADHD and not a personal deficit occurred when I was in my thirties and working in a community mental health center. Coincidentally, as such things always happen, a colleague started to talk one day about the condition and about working with children with ADHD. I had come across the term in the course of my studies, but had never had the opportunity or reason to look into it in any detail. Miran accepted me the way I was, without asking why I was so impulsive and headstrong, and the subject of ADHD had never been brought up between us. All the questions I still asked about why I had been so very unhappy as a boy and young man remained unanswered, and I had had no reason to think that this would ever change. Until now.

That evening, I brought one of Russell Barkley's books home to read, thinking that I probably would not get around to doing so, as is usually the case when I decide to read something. Barkley is one of the most important scholars of ADHD, and a leading proponent of the responsible use of medication in treating the condition. Almost single-handedly, he has been responsible for vastly increasing public and professional understanding of the disability. He certainly brought about great changes in my life.

It is usually hard for me to read a whole book in one sitting, but this time I tore through the pages, even forgetting to leave the study and eat.

Shortly after my conversation with my colleague, I received news that Barkley was going to give a seminar about ADHD in the area, and I decided to attend. This was my road to Damascus, when everything just "fell into place". On the podium, Barkley ran through case study after case study of typical children with ADHD. He could have been describing my early years and I was rigid with attention as I listened.

As I learned more and more about ADHD, the realization that I have the condition, and have had it for as long as I can remember became increasingly clear. I had not been an incorrigibly bad child, youth and young man – I had been struggling with an unidentified, untreated developmental disorder! Finally, I went to my family physician and told him my story. He peered at me over his bifocals, and said, “So you’re telling me that you have ADHD.”

“That’s right,” I answered.

“Very well then,” he asked me. “What kind of medication do you want?” He took out his prescription pad and pen and sat poised to write. He is a fine doctor, but he did not have any options to discuss other than drugs. Truth be told, the average physician knows so little about ADHD in adulthood that he has few options at his disposal, and in this my doctor was no exception. Research into the effective treatment of adult sufferers of ADHD is sparse, leaving even specialists of development disorders at a disadvantage when it comes to providing treatment. Ultimately, they have to fall back on what we know from research into the treatment of children and adolescents, which is not exactly ideal. Adult bodies quite simply do not process medications in the same way as children’s.

At first, I started taking Ritalin, the classic ADHD drug. It made me feel terrible. I had headaches and disorientation and I felt depersonalized, that feeling you get when you take way too much antihistamine and can’t quite make personal contact. I had all the side-effects. I tried Adderall and Concerta too, but they did not help a lot, either. Finally I tried the old favorite of Western medicine, Prozac. I hated them all and decided on a personal and on a professional basis, that medication was not the right way for me to go.

First, a disclaimer. The general practitioner that I attended was a good doctor. He provided me with the treatments recommended at that time and in fact I credit him for single handedly saving my father’s life on more than one occasion. But what kind of an assessment did he give me when I presented myself in his office for treatment? None at all. He did not ask me about when the disorder first became apparent, how I was so sure that I had it or whether or not I was interested in exploring non-medicative ways of treating it. He reached straight for his prescription pad. As I see it, it was also quite improper to start giving me medication with such a free hand. My stance on medication is that there are times when it is necessary, and that at all other times it should not be taken. The decision as to whether or not to take medication should *always* be subject to a detailed cost-benefit analysis and this had most certainly not been the case here.

My experimentation with drug treatments lasted for about a year. None of them worked, and I realized that, in my case, adjustments in the way I lived would provide a better treatment. The first step was to start by talking about the condition to the people I was closest to, my wife, my immediate family and my friend Jim. Earlier, I described my change of name from "Dick" to "Richard", together with the decision to attend college, as a sort of rebirth. This was a second new start.

Most people with ADHD still manifest symptoms of the condition in adulthood, although many not exactly as they did when they were children and adolescents. I certainly do, and the problems that arise from this are something that I have to struggle with on a daily basis. My infamous tendency to speak before thinking is still in place and can be embarrassing for others, like when my wife and I joined my brother and his wife for a skiing vacation. We were all taking the ski-lift uphill when a stranger approached and asked if he could share. "No," I told him. "I don't want to share with you." As usual, my gut reaction was the one that was voiced, as inevitably happens with people with ADHD. I did not stop to compose a more tactful way of suggesting that he travel separately, and I did not suppress my immediate feelings ("I don't know you. I don't think I like you. Go away."). Of course, my brother's wife was horribly embarrassed by what she perceived to be my outrageously impolite behavior, and yet another one of Richard's *faux pas* was written into Kuendig family lore.

In making frequent blunders of this kind, I am very typical of the ADHD adult. ADHD continues to damage the lives of adults in a number of important ways, predisposing vulnerable individuals to marital discord or general problems with relationships, a lack of organization, difficulty with holding onto jobs and an overall difficulty with concentration. As in the case of children and adolescents, the presence of ADHD in no way reflects the intellectual ability and aptitude of the individual, who frequently performs well below expectation, considering their general levels of intelligence. While some people have been diagnosed as children, and have grown up dealing with ADHD, others are diagnosed as adults. This can cause a variety of reactions, from relief at finally understanding the problems that have seemed to dog them throughout their lives, to distress. Undiagnosed ADHD adults may have developed a range of coping mechanisms over the years, helping them to minimize the impact of ADHD on their lives or, conversely, they may have turned to self-medication of a sort, such as a dependence on alcohol and/or other drugs or self-destructive behavior. In worse-case scenarios, their destructive tendencies are turned not only against them but also against their families and those around them.

Many of the adults with ADHD whom I encounter professionally are first diagnosed when the problem is identified in their child. They find changing their own behavior difficult, and often actively refuse to participate in systems designed to modify their behavior and reactions: “Don’t try to change me. I can’t change. This is the way I am. This is who I am.” Because my client is the child, my priority is that another young life is not marred by untreated ADHD and I always do my best to ensure that parents with ADHD start dealing with it, as part of the healing process for the whole family. Having a developmental disorder should never be a source of shame. Do not make the mistake of supposing that childhood agonies do not have a negative impact on the feelings of the adult, either. Just to illustrate this point, let me tell you a story from my own recent experience.

In early November, 2002, my friend Jim and I spent a Saturday afternoon riding our all-terrain vehicles, having a grand time splashing in the mud. As the evening began to approach, we decided to drop into Friday's for a cheeseburger and a margarita. We changed our clothes and, as we hadn't gotten very dirty, I decided not to take a shower. I washed up quickly, and we were on our way. Now, my hair tends to be a little wild, especially when it is wind-blown as it was after an afternoon of ATV riding. As we left, I grabbed a baseball hat and threw it on in a vain attempt to tame my very wild hair. I was reminiscent of Larry of the Three Stooges, with hair that almost exploded around my hat, standing out at a firm ninety degrees. Any clown would have been envious. Anyway, Jim and I sat quietly at the bar in Friday's for just long enough to finish our cheeseburgers and drink a single margarita each. Leaving, we had to walk past a group of adults, who seemed to be having fun, drinking beer, joking and laughing. Jim went through first, and as I followed I passed a woman who looked like she was in her early thirties and was quite attractive.

"Nice hair," she said aloud as I went by. In an instant, all the years of being teased and belittled returned to me. All the pain, humiliation and self-questioning were back. I stopped walking and turned to look at the lady (using the term in its more general sense), with every intention of finally dealing with a lifetime of having been victimized. As I looked at her, I felt helpless again. Afraid that if I stood up for myself, I would again be seen to be a wrong doer, a perpetrator of evil. Once again, I was the victim with no place to hide, and nowhere to seek refuge.

Outside, I told Jim what had happened (he had not heard her comment).

"Fuck her!" he said. I knew what he meant. "Blow her off. She's not important. Don't waste your time worrying about somebody like that." But when he said "Fuck her!" all I could hear were the voices of the teachers who had told me, for years, that I had somehow been the cause of whatever problem was occupying their attention, and that I could do nothing to improve the situation except perhaps, in this case, cut off all my hair.

People's inhumane treatment of each other is often at its worst when it is thoughtless rather than purposeful. When we become thoughtful towards others' needs as our worlds collide, love and humanity are able to create compassion and understanding. Those of us with ADHD often have the compassion to be understanding of others. Unfortunately, our differences often tempt others to behave with marked cruelty.

14
Helping ADHD Adults Be Grown-Ups

Fortunately, although there is still quite a way to go, attention is at last being turned to the topic of how we can best treat adults with ADHD. A crucial first step is to ensure that the adult in question really *has* ADHD and not another condition with similar symptoms which mimic the disorder. The physician or treating psychologist needs to be sure that the disorder was first manifested in childhood, and should speak at length with the patient about his early years. Ideally, the assessing professional should have contact also with members of the patient's family, who can give an objective assessment of his/her early behavior. Once a positive identification of the disorder has been made, treatment can begin. In children and adults, the dopamine receptors in the brain seem to be crucial in treating ADHD which is why, broadly speaking, the stimulant medications are apt for both. The research indicates that longer-acting stimulants have the greatest effect, although adult reactions to medication are markedly less consistent than those of children. Adults appear more sensitive to the medications than their juvenile counterparts and, more often than not, actually require *less* medication than children. I need to be clear about this point; it is not that some mystical medical process has taken place in adults that renders them more sensitive to the medications. Instead, adults are probably more self-aware than children, causing them to be more aware of the effects of the stimulant medication. Combined with the increased willingness of the adult to utilize social intervention this facilitates greater medical efficacy and treatment success. Some adults are often successfully treated with non-stimulant medication. In the absence of well-researched criteria for which prescription works best in adults, a degree of trial and error and, of course, patience, is required in finding the right treatment for the adult sufferer. A relatively new drug, Atomoxetine or Strattera, has been shown to work for significant numbers of adults with ADHD.

While both men and women can have ADHD, the numbers of males with the condition is still higher than females, as in childhood. In some ways, the disability is harder to deal with for men, as our culture is deeply intolerant of male emotion and feeling and the expression of the same. It took me many years to understand that a man's tears are a perfectly valid expression of sorrow.

Women with ADHD often seem initially to be depressed rather than hyperactive in any way, making the diagnosis of ADHD difficult. In our society, women are still largely responsible for childcare, and ADHD mothers can wreak havoc with their child's progress and their own state of mental well-being if they are left without the treatment and support that they require. They are inconsistent parents, find it hard to follow through with behavioral management systems, to remember to medicate their child at the right time, and to handle their own anger. I treat a 36 year old mother and her son, both of whom have ADHD. She has devised a wonderful, albeit ineffective, means of remembering to take her medication (she takes Strattera and her son takes Dexadrine). Since both of them find it very difficult to remember to take their medicine, they made a pact to remind each other. As good and mutually supportive as this idea is, the only problem is that one bad ADHD memory times one bad ADHD memory equals no memory at all for details.

When parents with ADHD see that they are failing, their anger tends to turn inward, leaving them depressed, confused and even more likely to be inadequate but well-meaning parents. As a psychologist, when I meet a mother with undiagnosed ADHD, my first step is to address her problems with organization, structure and the need for routine in an effort to solidify the foundation that the ADHD child is depending on, rather than the child's. It might even be that the child's behavior is worsened because he or she is reacting to his mother's inconsistency, mood swings and unpredictable use of punishment. Having lived a lifetime without the treatment they need, some of these women are full of suppressed anger, and are making life miserable for both themselves and their offspring.

Adult men with ADHD, like boys, are more likely to present an obvious and disruptive tendency towards impulsivity and hyperactivity. At its nastiest, this can be a contributory factor to physically violent behavior towards their wives, children or others. More often, it is expressed in the habitual blurting out of inappropriate remarks, the failure to handle money sensibly and difficulty in controlling anger. Again, the male parent's problems can have an extremely disruptive effect on the well-being of the whole family, as mother and children learn to dread Dad's rages, bouts of irrational temper and even violent outbursts. In order to instigate a successful treatment program for the child, Dad is going to have to come to terms with his own problems first and this is very often a monumental task. I call men "cement heads" because of their general tendency to view the world in very concrete terms, especially when it comes to parenting ADHD children. ADHD children (and most other children for that matter) quite clearly behave differently for men than they do for women. I wish I had a dime for every time I saw a family where the father loosely blamed the mother for the problems with their child when he said "I don't have any trouble with him at all, she just needs to be harder on him." His assumption that the child behaves "differently" for him is correct, but his demand that the mother just be harder on him is both impossible and inappropriate. Being a man he, obviously possesses a certain number of attributes including strength, a loud, low voice and a set of testosterone-driven behaviors that influence behavior in ways that the mother never will. Add this to the fact that, even in the 21st century, mothers are the primary care givers and you have the ingredients for problems in interparental consistency. We know that children with ADHD do well in novel situations, in situations that are one-on-one and in situations that involve men. Since the mother is the primary care giver, she never finds herself in these situations, while the father almost always does. Then, to make matters worse, since the mother is with the children more than the father, the kids quickly get used to her scariest demand, which barely compares to those that Dad will make when he gets home! Oh yes, my mother and her yard stick were almost as much entertainment as teasing my sister. But when my mother uttered the words, "I am going to tell your father," I quickly changed my tune from laughter and taunts to pleads for clemency. Mom often comforted me with the words, "I am not going to tell your father … this time."

The night I had my appendix out, I also had the misfortune of having to present Mom and Dad with one of my countless bad report cards. It was filled with "F's" and seventh grade had not been a greater success than past grades. But on that fateful night Mom realized that I might actually be sick.

"I think he is really sick," she said to Dad, who responded in a very impulsive, testosterone-influenced manner, saying, "I know what is making him sick. This report card is making him sick and I am going to beat the sick right out of him!"

No, my dad never really "beat" me, but he did not believe I was sick that night – not until I had an emergency room rectal exam confirmed case of appendicitis! I ended up in the operating room that very night and escaped the wrath of an ADHD father. In all honesty, however, I would not recommend that as a means of getting out of being punished for bad grades!

Are the differences in the way that ADHD is manifested in men and women biological or cultural in nature? Both, probably, but the bottom line is that the basic symptoms of the condition are present in men and women, and both need help. Disability and despair are qualities that are without gender.

Adults with ADHD, like their younger counterparts, tend to have high levels of creativity, energy and drive, as well as the potentially destructive aspects of the condition. These characteristics are all clearly of great benefit in many working environments, so why do so many men and women with ADHD find it hard to progress professionally?

The workplace is a potential minefield for adults with ADHD. Most jobs involve a great deal of tedious, routine work, and they do not have the means to handle boredom. They speak their mind and tell people when they are angry or frustrated, even if those people are their work superiors, and can dismiss them from their jobs. They argue with co-workers, turn up to work late, fail to be diplomatic in situations demanding tact and generally find themselves moving from one job to another, as my father did throughout his life. ADHD workers can also bring high levels of inspiration and spontaneity to the workplace, but their unreliability generally cancels out the positive effects of this. My father built a great career as a business consultant, but when he made the transition to President and CEO of big corporations, he was in constant and consistent contact with people who made daily demands. Having ADHD, he embarked on a spiral of failure. Dad was just not able to maintain consistent mental effort or remain on task long enough to perform up to the standards his position demanded. He was absolutely capable of managing the high level jobs he had but, unfortunately, he reached his ADHD induced level of incompetence prematurely and eventually lost everything he had worked for all his life.

As usual, one of the biggest problems here is (was) a lack of understanding of ADHD and a failure to diagnose it and instigate ways to compensate. The adult who has ADHD (my father in this case) and has not been diagnosed will not understand why chaos seems to rule only *his* life. He resents authority, acts impulsively and does not know how or when to apply the brakes, even if he could. He does not realize that, as he has unmanaged ADHD, *he* is usually the problem, and sees the world as a cruel place, in which employers and authority figures are usually "out to get him". If the condition is recognized and understood, the same symptoms are present, but coping mechanisms can be introduced.

Adults with ADHD, like their younger counterparts, are entitled to request that certain provisions be made for them in the workplace, to enhance their capacity to be productive and minimize the potentially destructive effects of their condition. Mindless discrimination against workers with ADHD is, of course, unforgivable and illegal. Anyone with a disability of any kind is entitled in our country to have provisions made to cope with the potential problem. However, this does *not* mean that the adult worker with ADHD should use the condition as an excuse for his every shortcoming, and expect someone else to pick up the tab. Keeping a disability perspective, let us compare the situation to that of the physically disabled worker who needs to use a wheelchair. He should expect his employers to provide him with a ramp so that he can enter the workplace, with special washroom facilities, and with a desk and office furniture adapted to his situation. Doors should be wide enough for him to move through, and there should be an elevator so that he can access the various floors in the building. However, if he comes into his specially equipped office every morning and spends the day writing emails to his friends, browsing the Internet, working on his novel or playing solitaire on his computer, should he be treated differently to everybody else? Absolutely not. His disability does not entitle him to do whatever he wants and then blame his situation. In this case, the playing field has been leveled for him and it is up to him to fulfill his end of the bargain. The same is true of people with ADHD. Demanding special provisions beyond what is reasonable is not just unfair, it is counterproductive for all people with developmental disabilities. The bottom line? Know your legal rights, make sure that they are fulfilled, and then do everything you can to live up to your end of the agreement. Show the world (and more importantly, yourself) that a diagnosis of ADHD is not a ticket to failure.

15
Living With ADHD

When children look at adults, they see huge, omnipotent beings who always seem to know what to do, and who speak with the voice of authority at all times. But when each of us grows up, there is always that moment when we ask ourselves, “Is this it? This is what being a grown-up is all about? But I still don’t know my place in the world!” Being an adult is about being responsible for oneself, and a part of that is the acceptance of one’s own weaknesses and shortcomings.

The adult with ADHD cannot use his condition as an excuse for all of his shortcomings. He must accept it, make special provision for it, and should ask for accommodations to made in the workplace, when necessary. He might reasonably ask those around him to be prepared to be especially patient and tolerant with him at times. But, like all adults, he must learn to be responsible in what ever way is demanded by the situation he or she is in. ADHD should never be used as an excuse for abusive, anti-social or otherwise destructive behavior. Having a greater understanding of ourselves is about working to make ourselves as good as we can be while accepting our limitations in certain areas, not about asking the world to give us a free ride! That said, it should be borne in mind that ADHD proper never *begins* in adulthood, it simply continues to be present in the individual who has been affected since childhood.

Although ADHD in children has been formally recognized and treated for some time, the same is not true of adults. Until relatively recently, the official consensus was that ADHD was a disorder of childhood and sometimes adolescence, with symptoms disappearing in adulthood. Unfortunately, in my opinion, this is not the case. In fact, at least two thirds of all children with ADHD continue to present with symptoms of the disorder in adulthood and those who do appear to be unaffected probably seem so because the condition is being properly managed, (and remember that "managed" can also mean that the life situation of the individual fits the needs of ADHD) not because it has "gone away". The tendency to underestimate ADHD in adults is closely linked to the fact that the most immediately obvious aspect of the disorder, hyperactivity, tends to diminish with the years or at least to respond most to conditioning on the part of the individual. While children with ADHD may actually get up from their chairs and rush around the room, the adult is more likely to find himself distracted by a wish to do so, or to repress the urge into less striking forms of activity such as fiddling with items on a table, fidgeting and moving his feet and hands restlessly. A running joke I share with my patients is that I always have something in my hands to fool around with. Recently, I have had either a six pound medicine ball that I throw up in the air while talking or a more subtle piece of silly putty that keeps my need to fidget satiated. It is not uncommon for a patient or their parents to bring me a small gift of a toy to play with in recognition of my restless nature. Most recently, a delightful woman brought me a small figurine of the Hulk to keep me focused while we discussed her complicated life problems.

The gravity of having ADHD in adulthood should not be underestimated. As is the case with adolescents, the condition is strongly associated with a much higher rate of car accidents, injuries in general, drug and other substance abuse, alcoholism, job loss, sexually transmitted disease and unplanned pregnancy, erratic self-medication and abuse. Learning disabilities and a variety of psychiatric disorders are also much more likely to be present in the individual with ADHD. All of this clearly indicates that adult ADHD is a serious condition, from which sufferers can die when they become involved in events closely linked to the condition. This alone should be motivation to ensure that treatment is provided, but consider also the drain that untreated ADHD adults place on the state in terms of the provision of health services every time there is an accident, social services when families break down, prison spaces when crime seems more appealing than labor, and so on. ADHD adults are at risk but most are more than capable of being productive members of society if they are identified, properly diagnosed and treated. This does not, however, necessarily mean medication, since many adults want to avoid medical treatment.

In my case, I have been able to build a successful business and maintain it largely because of the efforts of my wife, Miran. Clearly, if I may be so bold, it is my clinical expertise that keeps the practice thriving and growing. However, Miran is the real backbone of the business; Miran organized the billing, she set up the patient schedule and figured out all the different insurance codes that I would have found totally intolerable. In fact, before Miran was an integral part of the practice, I used to forget to show up for the appointments. Yes, that is right, the doctor himself was the one who did not show up and some patients were, quite rightly, not happy with my seemingly careless attitude towards the care of their family. Miran makes sure that I make appointments on time, that bills are paid when they should be and that deadlines are met. I am blessed in finding in her a professional as well as a personal partner. Often, the ADHD sufferer will be successful not only due to their expertise in this field or that but because there is a person, a wife, a secretary or an understanding co-worker who builds a safety net into their life, a cushion that allows for the impact of ADHD, while still pushing them enough to facilitate success. Admittedly, this can lead to conflict in the relationship but the pay-off, at least for me, has been worth it.

Although ADHD is a psychological disorder, as well as a neurological one, having dealt a lifetime with the difficulties of the condition can generate psychological scars which can be painfully difficult to recognize and deal with. It is important for the adult individual to be able to accept himself the way he is, and not to enact self-destructive behaviors, or, even worse, violent behaviors because of internalized anger.

For me, finding my own peace involved working on my relationship with my parents. We had become a lot closer since I went to college and graduated with a doctorate. They were proud of me, and I was proud of having made them feel good about having me for a son. But there was still a lot of hurt between us. I knew that I had been a nightmare to deal with. The fact that much of my behavior was clearly attributable to my having ADHD was not an excuse for all the pain that I had put Mom and Dad through. Sure, they could have done a lot more to help me to cope with my disability – if they had known about it, which they did not. When I was a boy and Mom and Dad were parents of a large family there was little or no understanding of ADHD and how it works. With their limited resources (not to mention the fact of Dad's own impulsivity) they had done their best. On the other hand, I found it difficult to let go of all the pain that had been caused by treatment that was objectively unfair and had made my ability to deal with my condition worse than it should have been. Fortunately, we had time to put everything to rights between us and my relationship with my parents throughout their final years was a good, and even a rewarding one!

After both Mom and Dad passed away, Bill, my oldest brother remarked on how I had been as upset as the rest of them at their funerals, saying, "It's not surprising, considering how close you'd become in recent years, but it is very surprising when you look at the earlier times."

I thank God that we were granted the time and opportunity to become close. Despite everything.

16
Status Quo

> *"Richard is full of love. The problem is that he doesn't realize it. He is always too hard on himself"* – Miran Kuendig.

Adults with ADHD are more likely than anyone else to experience marital discord and divorce. They don't make for easy spouses. In my case, our marriage remains strong in large part because of my wife Miran's immense patience. We've had our battles, and she keeps me in line, but she tolerates my vagaries with a saint-like calm, as she sees large portions of our income disappear to buy yet another ride-on lawn mower, remote-control model helicopter or computer program that we really do not need. Once, I hid an expensive motorcycle in the garage for weeks before finally admitting to her that I had bought it. Boy, did I feel silly as well as guilty when I had to admit that

The Kuendig Family in Recent Years

not only had I bought a motorcycle I did not need, but that I had hidden it for weeks, like a kid with a guilty conscience.

Another issue is that of the chores that I promise I will do in our home. Miran knows that I will do the things she asks me to, in time. I am going to hang the blinds in the study, I really am, just as soon as I have a free moment. It is true that they've been waiting for two years to be put up … but I *will* do it. And I truly mean it, every single time I say it! In fact, I think I might get around to it just as soon as I finish writing this chapter. Or maybe not. Be that as it may, the largest misconception I encounter, as a person with ADHD belief that when I say I will do something and then do not it, I never intended to do the task in the first place. I have ADHD, I am not an idiot, and nor am I insincere. But I do have a disability that severely affects my ability to follow through on tasks. When I tell you that I will do something, I absolutely do mean what I say at the moment of saying it, and I am totally without reserve in my intention to follow through with my commitment. But how does one measure intention? The obvious answer is that we measure intention by looking at the behavior the intention refers to. I completely agree that intent is a standard by which one can measure action and come up with an expectation for future behavior. At the risk of coming close to making ADHD an excuse rather than an explanation, those of us with ADHD are influenced by the here and now to such an extent that the words that came out of our mouths a moment, an hour or a year ago become all but obsolete when they are influenced by present circumstances. OK, you may judge me by my words *and* my actions, so long as you never forget that when I tell you I will do something, it is not a ruse designed to manipulate you and it is not a dishonest statement even if it doesn't get done for quite some time. Do not judge me too harshly because of my disability because, with the right social support, like my unbelievable wife, I can grow and compensate for my shortcomings.

The basic symptoms of ADHD in adults are the same as those in children; inattention, a tendency towards hyperactivity, problems with following through on tasks to completion. All of this can be tremendously frustrating for the spouse of the person with ADHD, and they need to think carefully about whether or not they'll be able to cope with the condition before entering marriage. However, knowing when one marriage partner has ADHD, accepting this and working as a unit to cope with the condition (not change it or him) gives the couple a much, much greater chance of success than is the case when one partner in a relationship has undiagnosed, untreated ADHD. Has having ADHD affected my marriage? Of course it has. On the other hand, *knowing* that I have the condition, and knowing how I can work with my wife to minimize its negative impact is a thousand times better than having ADHD and not knowing it, or worse yet, ignoring it.

Miran knows that I am impulsive and has often doubted my ability to be faithful to her. I have always been faithful but for sure, I have not always managed to inhibit my tendency to flirt. As usual, the words leave my mouth before I have had time to think them through and assess the potential for hurt that they contain. And to be the spouse of someone who flirts is not comforting. One is always left with the lingering doubts: "If he can flirt without giving it more than a second thought, what else is he capable of doing? If he is prone to behavior in the absence of thought, why will he be loyal to the marriage and me? How can I tell when he is telling me the truth? I know that he is impulsive – why should I think that he is able to resist temptation?" I can only reiterate that people with ADHD can persist in effort over time when the rewards are tangible. In my case, being able to spend my days with the woman I love and adore is more than reward enough!

Although Miran is about to qualify as a psychologist, I know that it is hard for her to see me in a completely objective light, all of the time. A couple's relationship is a subjective one, by definition. When I am rude, impulsive or disorganized, she can cry, "Why aren't you just more responsible? Why are you doing this? Are you deliberately trying to annoy or upset me?" Intellectually, she knows that I would never deliberately try to hurt her. Emotionally, it is not always easy for a spouse to gain the distance necessary to realize this truth completely. When I spend our money on yet another toy, or computer program, or household gadget, she sighs, and shakes her head. She insists that all I have to do is decide to be more rational and organized, and then everything will fall into place. Is this her professional or her personal view? Her personal view, absolutely. On the other hand, she is the one who makes it possible for me to make it through life. *Every success* I've had as an adult is due in large part to her. She makes sure that I get to where I have to go on time, that tasks are completed and that I don't spend every dollar I earn on gadgets and toys.

One of the many major decisions that we have made as a couple was that we would not have children. In this particular instance, I led the way and Miran agreed with my wishes. I thought of the horrendous time my parents had raising me and, knowing that there is a high chance that a child of mine would also have ADHD, I did not feel up to the challenge. Do I regret not having a child? Well, I have never been a parent, so I do not know what I am missing. Friends and relatives tell me that having children is the most enriching experience there is, but it is one that I will never have and I am prepared to live with that commitment. Would I recommend that other ADHD adults abstain from having children? Absolutely not. That is a decision that each couple has to make separately. ADHD is a disability, but people with ADHD can be successful and, as difficult as life still is for people with the problem, there are more resources now to help, if the condition is diagnosed and these are made available. The most important thing is that the parents or potential parents enter a situation that may become difficult with their eyes open to the potential oceans of pain and suffering an ADHD child can bring. Denial is dangerous when an ADHD person is considering becoming a parent, and knowledge is power.

Adults with ADHD often display a high degree of careless cruelty. I say "careless" because their behavior is not planned, but born of chaos, internal disorder and a profound lack of self-esteem. They take their spouses for granted, just as I took my friends for granted in the past, and don't seem to understand that they have to give as well as receive. They lose their temper quickly, and find it hard to deal with family duties, such as tedious parties with the in-laws, or chores around the house. Of course, everyone finds aspects of family life difficult at times, but adults without ADHD have a special gift – they know how to pretend when it is necessary to keep peace. They may *think*, "Oh, boy, my in-laws are really boring. When can we finish up and get out of here?" but they don't actually *say* it. When people with ADHD experience a flash of anger with their spouse, they do not wait to calm down and rationalize the feeling before voicing it – they yell straight away. Of course, they are likely to stop experiencing the anger just as quickly as they started experiencing it, but for the object of the outburst, the hurt remains and so does the suspicion that the angry words are deeply felt. Women with ADHD may be less likely to lash out in anger, or at least less likely to cause serious damage when they do so, but they can be as cruel, irrational and impatient as their male counterparts, all of which can result in damage to the marriage and, even more gravely, to the children growing up in a family dealing with ADHD.

As always, the key to enhancing the ADHD adult's chances of a successful relationship with spouse and children is understanding the condition. The way things currently stand, too many adults are never diagnosed as having ADHD, or are only diagnosed when their child is found to have it. This ignorance leaves their families with no choice but to assume that their transgressions, carelessness and rudeness represent deliberate behavioral decisions. Some time ago, Miran and I went out to dinner with a local couple with whom we were friendly. I started to tease the man (a psychologist) and, without thinking about whether I was behaving appropriately in a fancy restaurant, I picked up my menu and swatted him on the back of the head. He stared at me, finished his meal as quickly as he could and hurried his wife out the door after offering a cursory good bye. We have never seen them again.

Recently, I heard the case of a father who has ADHD who went crazy on entering an amusement park with his family when he was told that he could not take foodstuffs into the park. Instead of sighing and accepting the rule, he threw everything they had brought with them at the wall, including the bottles of milk they needed for the baby. Because this man has not learned how to deal with his ADHD, he insisted on trying to rationalize his behavior: "The stupid woman at the gate made me so angry I had to throw all our food away …" Imagine how difficult it is for the spouse of an ADHD person to deal with this sort of reaction every day throughout their marriage, especially if the ADHD has not been diagnosed and she (or he) sees this behavior as deliberate.

One of the most frequent causes of discord in a marriage in which one of the spouses has ADHD is money. People with ADHD are the ultimate impulse shoppers. For them, a credit card can be a lethal weapon, as the house fills with decorative, useless objects that will never be needed, with expensive designer clothes that do not even fit, with cute toys that the dogs are just going to *love* … In order to avoid problems, it might be wise for the ADHD spouse not to have a credit card at all!

Given all the extra strain that is placed on the couple when a spouse has ADHD, it is unsurprising that rates of separation and divorce are much more frequent in these cases than among couples where neither partner suffers from the condition. More bad news? Well, yes and no. Although things have not magically become easier than they were before, public understanding of ADHD is growing, and adults with ADHD are, little by little, being diagnosed and seeking help more than before. As younger generations of ADHD sufferers grow up receiving the treatment they need, tomorrow's ADHD adults will be increasingly able to manage their symptoms and will know when to seek help. In short, with the correct attention and treatment, men and women with ADHD can make successful marriages and be happy adults.

Of course, adults with ADHD often have kids with ADHD, and this introduces a particular set of challenges, if the child is to receive the care he needs. One of the most important aspects of managing juvenile ADHD is training the parents in coping with the condition, and in introducing treatment strategies. These can be tiresome and difficult to remember at the best of times, and are especially challenging for the untreated ADHD adult, who can find the tedious duty of establishing a routine enormously difficult. Like their ADHD child, they are not good at following through on instructions or sticking to plans, and tend to switch treatment strategies "half way through", fail to be consistent with rewards and punishments, and argue with their children and with the treating physician or psychologist. In fact, ADHD children with ADHD parents have less successful treatment outcomes than those with normal parents.[7] In designing strategies to help ADHD children, caregivers need to think also about parents' strengths and weaknesses, and create systems that are viable within the structure of the given family. Failing to successfully implement a treatment strategy is damaging for the child, and negatively influences the parent's sense of self-worth, too.

---

[7] Sonuga-Barke, E. et al, "Does maternal ADHD reduce the effectiveness of parent-training for preschool children's ADHD?" *Journal of the American Academy of Child and Adolescent Psychiatry*, 41, 2002 696-701.

The best time for ADHD to be diagnosed is when the person with the condition is still a child, but it is never too late to start introducing ways to help with behavior modification and to work towards building a happier, more controlled future. Even the adult whose childhood and youth was marred by the disability, as mine was, can find greatly enhanced peace in recognizing the condition for what it is, in learning how to control it more, and in allowing it to impact negatively on those around him less.

What's my life like now? Well, as I grow older, I have come to terms with having ADHD, and with the fact that it is never going to go away. I will never be able to sit still during a movie, or even understand how other people can do so – not wriggle for more than an hour and a half? You have *got* to be kidding! When I give a seminar, I provide just as much of a visual display as an audio one, as I roam about the podium, sit down, stand up, fiddle with my Diet Coke can and decide whether or not I want to write on the blackboard to illustrate a point. In clinical terms, I would describe myself as having "managed ADHD". It has not gone away, but it no longer has a huge negative impact on my life. One thing that helps a lot is that I buy myself almost all the toys I need to keep myself amused (grown-ups need toys too, you know). But the person who really keeps me afloat is my wife Miran and the endless love she showers me with.

ADHD never goes away. I know that I have ADHD and that I always will have it. I could be resentful, but I am not. Not any more. What would be the point? We all need to accept who we are and what we're made of, and to make the best of our situation without anger. This acceptance, and the willingness to strive to be as good as we can, is what being an adult with or without ADHD is all about.

Acknowledgments

I thought long and hard about these acknowledgements before sitting down to write them. It is not easy to dedicate something that has so much meaning to one person or even a specific group of people when, after suffering from ADHD for such a long time, it still feels that the only reason I finished this was because of the incredible effort and unbelievable patience of those people in my life who have ever loved me. The people who pushed me and tolerated my unending procrastination are the ones who deserve the credit for this book because their effort and unending love are what made it a reality. Putting the words down on paper was much easier than believing in, loving and wanting the best for me, despite the agony my ADHD has caused.

Having ADHD is a many-faceted torture. Of course, there is the age-old problem of needing to be told what to do over and over again. Then there is the need to be reminded, countless times, of all the mundane things in life, those things which I routinely try to avoid in the first place! And let's not forget the agony I experienced every time I started a project and did not finish it … and then being reminded of the fact by what seemed like everybody on earth.

The real torture of ADHD is not caused by external factors, however, but comes from within my own heart. In writing this book, I was forced to recall many memories which opened deep emotional scars. Even now, I am reminded of the pain my inconsiderate, thoughtless behavior has often caused. It matters not at all that the hurt I caused the people I love so much was unintentional. The fact is that my thoughtlessness and lack of consideration created deep injury that words cannot even express. The true torture of having ADHD is the ability to empathize with the pain one causes, without being able to stop doing it.

This book's existence is due especially to three people, together with my deep sorrow and regret for all the wrongs that I have committed.

First, my father. Without the support he gave me throughout my life and his belief in me, I would not have learned how to overcome adversity. My father taught me many times that adversity does not mean that one's goals cannot be met, but that it is a fact of life, must be faced and can be overcome. Nobody welcomes adversity, but throughout his life my father demonstrated that when a storm hits your path, you are in charge; you can choose the direction you will take and you can direct your reality rather than allowing it to direct you.

Secondly, my mother. Mom was both a traditional woman from the old school and a revolutionary. She taught me old world values and new world adventures. She was strict with the rules, but also taught me the need for excitement and adventure. Somewhere between a liberal and a conservative, had my mother not had the perseverance to see through my thin veneer of chaos, I would never have learned how to go on loving when I was angry or how to see life through eyes full of hope and anticipation.

Finally, to the one person I have hurt the most and loved the most, I dedicate every word of this book and every tear I have shed.

When I married Miran fourteen years ago, I thought that I loved her and that she loved me. I was half right. The love I feel for Miran now dwarfs any feeling I have ever experienced. Miran has taught me the meaning of love, dedication and self-sacrifice. More than once, she has said that she should divorce me, and every single time she has demonstrated the meaning of commitment, dedication and devotion, by moving beyond the pain I created and allowing her love to shine in our marriage. As a man with ADHD, I am not easy to be married to, and if Miran did not have true love in her heart, I would not be married today. She has singlehandedly turned my chaotic, ADHD life into one of caring, giving and understanding. I owe Miran all that I am. Without her, all that I am is incomplete.

Appendix
The Nuts and Bolts of ADHD

This book has been written to give you insight into what it is like to grow up and live with ADHD, and not to describe how the condition should be treated. But it is important to know some basic information on the treatments available and the legal provisions that have been made for the condition. You may already have learned quite a bit about drug and other treatments in your personal quest to understand ADHD. If not, this will serve as an introduction. Bear in mind, however, that drug and other treatments are under continuous review. To find the best possible treatment for you or your child, you need to speak with an appropriately qualified, responsible health care provider.

Ritalin or methylphenidate, which is the generic form, is the drug most commonly used to treat children with ADHD – so much so, that the brand-name has widespread recognition among members of the public and even among children in grade school, who may identify Ritalin-taking classmates as targets for teasing and bullying. It is a stimulant medication which acts on the neurotransmitters in the brain that are, theoretically, under-active in individuals with ADHD. While it can take some trial and error to arrive at the perfect dosage level, Ritalin is used successfully in most cases, and side effects are relatively rare, especially in older children, apart from a minor reduction in appetite and occasional head or stomach aches. The positive effects include an increase in attention span, a reduction in fidgetiness, impulsive behavior and aggression and improved ability to focus. It should go without saying that any person diagnosed as having to take medication should be carefully monitored to ensure that they do not suffer adverse effects.[8] Much media attention has been given to Ritalin's

[8] Adverse effects particularly associated with Ritalin include palpitations,

potential for abuse. This generally occurs among college students, who see it as a useful aid to study. While the media never hesitate to exaggerate dangers of abuse, parents should certainly be vigilant to ensure that the drug ends up where it belongs. It is possible that some stimulant medications, such as Ritalin, may aggravate existing tic disorders such as Tourette's disorder in some individuals.

Unfortunately, because Ritalin has such widespread recognition in society, children who take the drug can be subjected to discrimination from their peers and even from teachers and other people in positions of authority. This can be one of the reasons why a child is prescribed a similar drug with a different brand-name and, if such bullying occurs, it is a valid one. It is hard enough to be a child with ADHD, without being treated as a social pariah in the classroom and the playground.

Like Ritalin, Dexedrine is a stimulant medication. It was originally developed in the 1920s to treat depression, but has been shown in clinical trials and medical practice to be effective in the treatment of ADHD, too. Dexedrine may be prescribed to patients who suffer negative side effects from taking Ritalin. Three quarters of the patients who are treated with Dexedrine improve while taking the drug although, while serious side-effects are rare, problems similar to those sometimes found with Ritalin may occur. Patients should certainly be monitored carefully, and it should be borne in mind that it can take some time to arrive at the "perfect" dose.

Adderall is related to Dexedrine, which was first marketed as a long-acting, once-a-day medication for ADHD. Unfortunately, like so many drug company promises, the hope of Adderall being a once-a-day medication did not come true. In

tachycardia, increased blood pressure, excessive CNS stimulation, psychosis, depression, dizziness, headache, insomnia, nervousness, irritability, worsening of Tourette's syndrome, anorexia, nausea, vomiting, stomach pain, dry mouth, weight loss, growth suppression, alopecia, blurred vision, leukopenia, skin rash, facial tics, ecchymosis and rebound problems.

testimony to that, the makers of Adderall released Adderall XR (extended release) in 2001, and said again that Adderall is now a once-a-day medication. At any rate, like Ritalin and Dexedrine, Adderall is a central nervous system stimulant that comes with all the same side effects as the rest of the stimulant medications. However, Adderall comes with one very specific side effect: rage. Yes, that is correct, I said 'rage'. Far from a typical temper tantrum, the rage I am referring to is noticeably larger and of greater intensity. Believe me, when you have a drug induced rage going on, you will see the difference! By the way, the literature claims that the occurrence of this exaggerated anger state is present in only about 8% of the people prescribed it. I should caution you, however, that the anecdotal experience with which I am familiar suggest higher rates, of around 30%.

Concerta is a reformulation of the well-known drug Ritalin, designed for a slower release into the patient's system, which means that the behavioral "peaks and valleys" that can occur with patients taking Ritalin are absent, and that in many cases, one pill per day is sufficient.

Metadate, like Concerta, is Ritalin under another name – a reformulation of the well-known drug for slow release, with similar benefits. Interestingly, however, Metadate is the only formulation that has actually been approved to be sprinkled in the food of the patient in case taking pills is a problem.

Again, Focalin is a reformulation of Ritalin, and is a central nervous system stimulant. Approved for use as recently as 2001, it has been shown to be effective in treating individuals with ADHD. It shows great promise in the treatment of ADHD. Administered orally, it prevents the reuptake of noradrenaline, which is implicated in concentration and control of impulsive behavior and has a good success rate among a high proportion of the population. It seems that its use may cause a degree of appetite suppression. Focalin is slightly different from the other formulations of Methylphenidate in that it has a single molecule removed, called an isomer, that is thought to be the cause of the common side effects in the other formulations of the same medication. The drawback of Focalin is that it is both very expensive and usually requires QID dosing (that is doctor talk for four times a day).

Desoxyn (Methamphetamine Hydrochloride) can be successfully used in treating ADHD, but doctors avoid giving it to vulnerable patients, as there is a relatively high potential for abuse and addiction, as is the case with widely-used drugs such as Ritalin and Dexedrine.

Cylert is also a stimulant medication which can be used in the treatment of ADHD. Although it can be very successful (three quarters of users register improvement), it is rarely a doctor's first choice, as taking the drug does entail more risk than the commonly used Ritalin and Dexedrine. Especially, people with liver disease or a family history of liver problems should not take the drug due to its tendency to elevate liver enzymes and cause liver damage

Tofranil, Nopramin and Prozac are not stimulant medications, but anti-depressants, which have been found to be effective in treating a proportion of individuals with ADHD, probably by enhancing the way in which neurotransmitters in the brain pick up information. Tofranil is especially useful in treating those who suffer from sleep disorders, mood swings or enuresis.

While people with AHDH frequently require medication to enable them to make the most of their abilities, medication alone is not enough to successfully treat the problem. Parents and other caregivers can activate various systems to encourage and help the ADHD child to learn how to manage inattentive and impulsive behavior, by initiating a system of reinforcing positive behavioral patterns with recognition and reward, rather than simply punishing the wayward child. In the home, parents can help to focus their child's attention by breaking chores or games down so that concentration for more than brief periods of time is not required. Clinical approaches such as EEG neurofeedback are also available.

What is neurofeedback? Well, it is a system that measures the brain's responses to stimuli, by means of electrodes attached to the patient's scalp. The "brainwaves" are processed through a computer, and represented in visual form. This allows the patient and doctor to understand what lies behind reactions and counter-reactions, and to create a system to help the patient attain a higher degree of control over his or her brain activity. The idea is fairly simple; if a person can control their neuro-activity, the brain process that dictates and mediates behavioral control, they will automatically be controlling their behavioral output. Normally, people cannot control what their brain is doing, per se. But when we put the actual brain activity on a computer screen, in real time, control of that activity can be learned and mastered.

Medication modifies behavior through the chemical manipulation of brain activity. Neurofeedback modifies behavior through the willful manipulation of one's own brain activity. Neurofeedback can be used to help patients who use medication to manage their ADHD symptoms, or in people who are unmedicated. From the point of view of the juvenile patient, treatment can be fun, and learning to modify thought patterns and reactions can seem almost like a game.

No treatment plan can work if behavior management is not an integral part. Inevitably, parents, teachers and caregivers find themselves operating under a system of problem prevention when it comes to managing the ADHD child: "Don't go there! Don't do that! Stop! Sit down! Be quiet!" Of course, the ADHD child's behavior often needs to be controlled to prevent him from hurting himself or others, or quite simply from causing chaos. However, more important than preventing disruptive or defiant behavior is the reinforcement of acceptable behavior. When the child does something good, approval should always be verbalized. The adult should not say, "It's nice to see you keeping out of trouble for a change," but "Well done! You did a great job!". What is important is that the child learn that, while his behavior may sometimes be unacceptable, he is not a bad person. When good behaviors are not acknowledged and recognized, there is little incentive to continue being good. Because it is objectively harder for children with ADHD to conform to behavioral norms, they may need praise for behaviors taken for granted in other youngsters. When the child does something bad, an admonishment should be accompanied by suggestions for alternative actions: "Johnny, stop doing that. Why don't you draw a picture instead? You draw so well." It is important for children to be socialized so as to be able to mingle with their peers without damaging themselves, others, or property, but the lesson that they have to take home is that they sometimes do bad things, not that they are bad people. The child who feels that he is already condemned because he is a "born troublemaker" has little reason to improve his behavior. He thinks, along with everybody else, that he is just a bad person, and that he cannot be good, even if he tries. To coin a phrase, he is damned if he does, and he is damned if he does not. This is clearly not the sort of message that we want our children to pick up if we hope that they will grow into happy, successful adults. My advice to parents is that they ensure that each admonishment is balanced with two positive remarks. From my own experience with ADHD, I know that positive reinforcement works. Most of my teachers in grade school and in high school saw me as an obstacle to their teaching, a problem that had to be dealt with. There was just one who actually saw me as an ordinary boy, the teacher who taught me English in high school. My English teacher saw me as a greater challenge than the other pupils in her class, for sure, but not as an inherently evil person who would be better out of the way. As a result, English was the only class I did not regularly flunk out of, because I actually preferred attending class to hanging out in the woods. I knew that when I made an effort to be good, my teacher would acknowledge it.

One of the problems that all ADHD people have is with structuring their time, and this is especially true of children. When parents and caregivers don't help with this issue, all sorts of time-related problems arise, from not getting assignments handed in when they should be, to staying up all night. Rather than allowing the child to designate his own timetable and organize his own homework time, parents and teachers should intervene by providing help and guidance in this matter. Visual aids can be very helpful, such as colorful timetables displayed in the area where the pupil attends to his home duties. Break homework into realistic time-slots, with regular breaks to run around, or have a snack. When the child knows that he only has to concentrate for ten minutes at a time, rather than attempting to take on the mountainous chore of homework in one fell swoop, dealing with the challenge becomes much more manageable and the outcome is much more likely to be a success.

All children, like all adults, are different. As I tell the parents who come to me for help with their offspring: "They don't come with a manual." Although medication and techniques to help children modify their behavior usually help enormously, there is no "one size fits all" approach. It is crucial to recognize the ways in which one child differs from another, and tailor treatments accordingly.

A word of caution to the consumer. Recently, there has been an upsurge, mostly on the part of neurologists and psychologists, to use computerized tests of vigilance to make a diagnosis of ADHD. These tests, the TOVA, or Test of Variables of Attention and the Connors Continuous Performance Test, measure a person's levels of impulsivity and their ability to stay on task when it is quite boring. The tests are twenty-two and fourteen minutes respectively and are supposed to be applicable to everyday life. In fact, although these computerized continuous performance tests are thoroughly researched, they are not able to pick out a person with ADHD from a crowd of other people. Nor are these highly-touted tests able to distinguish between a person with ADHD and one with Tourette's syndrome or Asperger's disorder. The public, dazzled by the fact that these tests are administered by experts in white coats, generally considers them to be absolutely reliable, but they are not. To further complicate matters, some neurologists perform what is known as a "challenge test", in which the patient is given a computerized continuous performance test like one of those mentioned above and then given a small dose of a stimulant medication, usually Ritalin. Once the drug has been administered, the test is given again to see if the results improve. The assumption is that if the results are better after medication has been taken, there is proof positive that the subject has ADHD, and that the medication will help them. The problem with this approach is that stimulant medications work for *everybody*, with or without ADHD. The fact that someone's performance on a computerized test improves after taking a stimulant proves nothing other than the fact that the medication really was a stimulant. Medications used in treating ADHD are not diagnostic tools and should not be used as such.

Consumer beware! Just because a given professional can write "M.D." after their name does not mean that they are an authority on ADHD. In fact, I believe that the many neurologists who administer these tests as definitive diagnostic tools are merely perpetuating the myth that tests can diagnose ADHD, while cashing in on the ill-placed mystique that still surrounds the medical community.

Many more boys than girls are diagnosed as having ADHD – the ratio is generally estimated to be at about 3 to 1, although certain cultural factors may result in more referrals of boys, and the figures may not reflect reality in a completely accurate way. My personal opinion is that the numbers of girls and boys with ADHD are probably quite equal in actuality, which would mean that a lot of girls are being passed over in diagnosis and are not receiving the recognition and treatment they need. In general, it seems that hyperactivity is more noticeably present in boys with the condition, while most little girls with ADHD present with inattention. My take on this is quite simply that boys have much higher levels of testosterone, a hormone that triggers active, aggressive and even destructive behavior. Girls' forms of hyperactivity and inattention are less disturbing to adults – are more likely to make the girls seem "daydreamy" or "not with it" – and are more frequently dismissed as being indicative of a child's lack of academic ability or concentration than a possible developmental disorder. If this is true, a lot of little girls are not being helped to achieve all that they might, simply because of our culture's black-and-white way of viewing gender difference. The ratio of diagnoses is much more equal in adulthood although, again, certain cultural factors may be influential. By and large, women are more amenable to seeking professional help for physical and mental health problems than men because they are much less likely to have been taught that seeking help is a sign of weakness. It is also fair to say that many boys with ADHD suffer more from bullying – both verbal and physical – than their female counterparts. Our society expects male children to "be able to stand up for themselves" and tolerates a much higher degree of unpleasant behavior towards them, while little girls are treated more protectively. Just like discrimination against women in the workplace, this attitude is a product of patriarchal society. We want our boys to be men when they are no more than children, and in need of just as much cherishing as their sisters. This attitude can be damaging for all male children, but most especially those who are vulnerable and need support.

Although girls and boys who have been diagnosed with ADHD receive the same treatments with respect to medication, other therapeutic techniques need to be adapted to gender differences (both innate and learned). Girls tend to be more verbal than boys, and from an earlier age, so treatments focus more on talking with them, explaining issues that they might not understand, and helping them to express their thoughts and reservations. Girls tend to respond to logic. A typical treatment plan for little boys is much more action-oriented, reflecting the fact that they are usually more boisterous than girls, are often less verbally developed, and tend to see the world in more simplistic terms. Needless to say, not every child fits neatly into gender stereotypes. Some little boys can be inattentive, and some little girls can be boisterous. Parents, teachers and medical or psychological professionals should take time to get to know what "makes the child tick" before forming rigid opinions about the best way in which to help him.

It has been established that ADHD is probably caused primarily by genetic factors, but parenting style has a significant impact on the likelihood of a successful outcome in treating and managing the condition. There is no cure, but the individual's likelihood of succeeding or failing in life is greatly influenced in early childhood. In short, there are parents who are counterproductive to their child's development and the process of learning to deal with ADHD, just as there are parents who can provide an active, positive input. Criticism about the way in which one rears a child can hurt – but it is better to accept that parenting can be modified and improved than to continue down a destructive path. An imperfect parent is not a monster – he or she is perfectly normal. It is the willingness to adapt that makes one a good parent. Admitting that you are not perfect is not a display of weakness, but of strength. You have probably heard of men who would rather drive around lost for hours than pull up and ask for directions. Many Moms' and Dads' approach to parenting is exactly the same. They just do not want to acknowledge that there are times when they do not know what to do. One type of parenting problem I frequently encounter is the case of the high-achieving couple. You know the type – highly educated, motivated, earning high salaries and using every opportunity to display their intellectual prowess. There is nothing wrong with that. The problem lies in the fact that such parents often have a particularly hard time accepting and dealing with their child's ADHD. They see it as reflecting badly on the paradigm of perfection that they have created for their family. The child's problems with schoolwork, discipline and interaction with his or her peers are seen as damaging the image of the parents and the family as a whole. Moms and Dads with this attitude either deny the problem or lack patience, and want their child to perform to their standards of excellence. When they bring their child for treatment, they want instant results. All parents must understand that there just is not a single model for success. Academic training and educative techniques must be flexible, and parents and educators must be able to recognize different forms of achievement. Children who are not very academic at school often catch up later, or succeed in practical, artistic or technical fields. Children who can't make the ball team can do something else, instead. Some people will never be good at math, no matter how hard they try. Your children are *not* extensions of yourselves. Their weaknesses are their challenges, not yours, and their triumphs belong to them. As parents, your responsibility is to help them be all they can, not to try to force them into a rigid behavioral model of your own devising.

A problem with anger management is another frequent aggravator of ADHD in a child, and this is a situation I most commonly see when a parent – usually the mother, because mothers are still usually the primary caregivers – is suffering from depression. Depression generates high levels of intolerance, clearly unhelpful in dealing with difficult children. In these cases, the first step of treatment has to be addressing the emotional issues affecting the parent, and recommending medication when necessary. There have been times when the first course of treatment I have undertaken for the betterment of an ADHD child has been to advise the mother to see a physician and discuss the possibility of taking medication for her own problems. In my own family, I know that Mom was often overwhelmed by the responsibility of caring for her large number of children, at least one of whom had ADHD. She didn't need medical treatment, but I am sure it would have been helpful for her to have had the opportunity to talk things through with a caring professional.

An important issue of parent-child interaction is the fact that, as ADHD has a large genetic component, kids with ADHD often have parents who also suffer from the condition, even if it remains undiagnosed. This can lead to a wide range of problems. A parent can become angry and irrational when he recognizes his own childhood problems being recreated in his offspring, or the symptoms of ADHD can impact negatively on the parent's ability to administer medication regularly to the child, or to systematically follow a program of behavior modification. In worst-case scenarios, ADHD parents have even taken their child's medication for themselves. Perhaps most often, the parent denies that there is anything wrong with his child, saying that he is "just like me when I was that age," as if that made everything alright. All of this indicates clearly the importance of early diagnosis, and of social and personal acceptance of ADHD as a disability. Any treatment program must be designed for the whole family, and not just the child with the diagnosis.

ADHD children are often defiant, and it is crucial that parents maintain a firm sense of authority. It is *not* abusive to restrain your child to his or her room when you have to deal with tantrums, or to refuse to capitulate to the child's demands. A degree of any child's "acting up" is a way of testing the boundaries of acceptable behavior in the various social circumstances in which he finds himself. If those boundaries are not shown to him, he will never learn to adapt his reactions appropriately. A failure to maintain and instigate authority is detrimental to the child's development as a happy, functional member of society and is unfair to him. If he has only recently learned how to dress himself, how can he be expected to have the intellectual and emotional capacity to make an important moral and practical decision? That has to be the parents' responsibility. The key point to bear in mind is that disciplinary actions must be implemented only when it is fair to the child. Do not punish him because his disability causes him to be unable to do something, but when he *is* able, and still refuses. As a small boy, I was constantly punished for writing messily, something which was beyond my control, because of my poor fine motor coordination. Needless to say, the chastisement had no effect on my handwriting, and a lot on my attitude – not to mention being an endless cause of frustration for Mom and Dad who had to look over page after page of unreadable scrawls and deal with an angry, resentful little boy.

Some ethnic groups have very low rates of diagnoses for ADHD. Why is this? Not because less children in the group have the condition, but because the culture has very low tolerance for ADHD type behaviors, and has "built-in" behavioral mechanisms that work with a high rate of success in the case of the children who would otherwise be disruptive and out of control, or, conversely, because the culture does not identify the symptoms of ADHD as problematic. The fact that the children of many ethnic minorities are not diagnosed is far from encouraging. Instead of receiving the treatment they need, these individuals are even more likely than their majority counterparts to drop out of school early and fail to live up to their capabilities, being restrained both by their disability and by their minority status. A commitment to equality in our society entails making sure that all vulnerable individuals are identified early and provided with the treatment or treatments they need, regardless of their physiognomy, the color of their skin, their first language or their postal address. In our culture, many ethnic minorities already have to "do better" than other people in order to be treated equally. They do not need to have deal with the extra burden of having an undiagnosed, untreated disability.

Children with ADHD do not live in a social vacuum. While the condition is probably based in genetic, physiological factors, the social and familiar environment in which they grow up influence profoundly their chances of succeeding at managing their symptoms, conquering the challenges of schoolwork and becoming happy, successful adults and able parents in their own right. Adults who blithely assume that children are oblivious to their surroundings and the relationships between the adults in their lives are delusional, and although ADHD children may not be able to sit still for long enough to verbalize their feelings and reactions to tension and stress, this does not mean that they are not influenced by them.

Divorce can be very difficult for *all* children, and while the adults' traumas often wash over the ADHD child, who is just too busy to sit down and take notice, some experience the classic self-accusation even more profoundly than children without a developmental disorder. They blame themselves for the death of their parents' marriage. Why? Sadly, many ADHD children are told, either explicitly or non-explicitly, that the marital breakdown *is* their fault. If only they had been more manageable and less difficult, this would never have happened! This is not the sort of burden that any child should have to carry, and will in no way serve to modify the ADHD child's behavior for the better. Instead, it will teach them that they and not their behavior are bad. That they are incorrigible. That there is nothing they can do to make things better, because they are already damned by their circumstances: "If I'm so bad that I made Mom and Dad fight and separate, how will I ever learn how to sit still and do my homework? There isn't even any point in trying! Life sucks!"

Divorce is often marked by bitterness and anger, and it is inevitable that some of this will spill over and affect the children of the marriage. While adults can be very absorbed by their own problems at this time, they must remember to soothe the fears and doubts of their offspring. If their child has ADHD, he may need special reassurance that, although his parents may get angry and impatient at times, the divorce is *not* his fault. Parents must continue to display a united front and to cooperate in providing the child with the support and help with behavior modification that he needs. If this calls for attending meetings with the child's psychologist or teachers together, so be it. For better or worse, divorced parents will be linked for so long as their child needs them, if they have any sense of responsibility at all. As teenagers are all too prone to yell, they did not ask to be born! It is a parent's duty to give his child all the help he needs in becoming a well-rounded individual.

Children with ADHD are particularly vulnerable to growing up with poor scholastic records, and to developing an alcohol or drug-related problem, teen pregnancy or sexually transmitted disease. All of this can be mitigated by providing effective treatment and educational strategies early in life. Remember that ADHD is a condition which first appears in children before the age of seven. Clearly, just to be cold-blooded for a moment, these people are going to cost the government a lot less money if they are helped when they are young, rather than incarcerated, punished and provided with medical treatment later on. Common sense suggests that investing in these children when they are in grade school would be a wise step for our government to take. But what really happens? The sad truth is that ADHD treatment is not covered by Medicaid, America's half-hearted answer to socialized medicine. Low-income families who wish to submit their children for treatment have nowhere to turn, and a large percentage of these children become casualties of an uncaring society. Let me be blunt for a moment. If you take any given sample of underage prostitutes, drug addicts or juvenile violent criminals, you will find that their incidence of ADHD is much higher than in the general population. This is not because these young people were "born bad". It is because they were born with a *problem* and their families, their teachers and our society did nothing to help them to overcome it. Their inability to succeed reflects badly on us all. Given the genetic component of ADHD, these problems are often intergenerational, and are frequently complicated by factors such as parental alcohol abuse or violence and more. As things stand, we run the risk of creating an entire sub-class of people with unmedicated, unmanaged ADHD. Without recognition, treatment, and help, they will turn to self-medicating themselves with illegal drugs, and the inevitable drug-related problems of crime, violence and community disorder will arise. Is this really what we want? We all deserve more.

The families of children with ADHD may initially meet with apparent willingness to help from their child's educators, or they may be unlucky enough to meet with hostility from the very start. Sadly, many schools are not prepared to go the extra mile in helping vulnerable pupils. It is important to know that there are certain minimal legal rights which belong to the student with ADHD. The Individuals with Disabilities Education Act of 1997 (IDEA), section 504, recognizes ADHD children[9] as being "other health impaired" and acknowledges that they are eligible for special education services if they need them. If you must, gently remind the authorities in your child's school that there are laws to protect the ADHD child. If time passes, and no help is given, let yourself be more insistent. People with ADHD do need special help at times, and now they are legally entitled to it. Unfortunately, interpretation and application of the relevant laws do leave room for vagueness and

[8] For the purposes of the act, considered as being individuals from the age of 3 to 21

personal opinion. Fight for what you know to be right. You can, if necessary, file a complaint with the US Department of Education or with the Office of Civil rights, if your school is ignoring the needs of your ADHD child. You can call for a multidisciplinary meeting at which the legal issues and the implications for your child will be discussed. If this happens, remember to ask for a copy of the notes of the meeting, bring someone with you to provide support and act as a witness and make sure that you are clear about your needs. There is no reason for you to be apologetic. You are a tax-payer, your child has a disability and he has certain legal rights that must be fulfilled by the school. Children with disabilities that impact on their ability to learn at school are, in theory provided with "individual education plans" or IEPs, which are designed to maximize their chances of mastering schoolwork. Parents should not be satisfied with schools which suggest that there is a "one size fits all" individual education plan. Any plan should be what it is intended to be; individual. While some strategies may work for many children, all plans should be carefully devised and tailored to suit the person they are designed for. Once a child has been formally recognized as having a developmental problem, the school must provide services, and these services cannot be withdrawn without notifying parents. If the parents object, the services must continue unless the school can prove that they are no longer necessary. Before the educational plan is put in place, changed or withdrawn, the school must arrange to have a multi-disciplinary meeting with the parents of the child in question. Parents can make sure that these meetings are as effective as possible by preparing themselves. They should be ready and able to explain ADHD and its consequences for the individual in question, perhaps to the extent of preparing photocopies or handouts which explain the condition to provide to skeptical teachers. While it is not wise to enter meetings in a confrontational mood, there is no need to be apologetic, either. Understand that specialized education is the right of the child and that the law is on his side. Assure educators that the family is willing and prepared to put behavior modification systems into place in the home, and that the child's problem is being taken seriously and addressed. Being polite, but firm and confident, is the best way to make teachers understand and empathize. Sadly, it cannot be assumed that the school will take accurate notes of the meetings, so parents should be ready to take their own notes, and even record the meeting if necessary. A copy of the school's notes should be provided to parents. Under no circumstances should educators confuse parents, either deliberately or through carelessness, by using jargon or abbreviations that cannot be understood by the layman. If something is not understood, or is imperfectly understood, ask for clarification and do not feel ashamed for doing so. Specialists in any field, from education to agriculture, have specialized vocabularies that may not be accessible to other people. Bring a companion to the meeting for moral support and to assist with note-taking and questions. If the time allotted for the meeting expires before all of the issues have been addressed, ask to reconvene. If the school refuses, ask them to put their refusal and the reason for it in writing. As a final step, it is always possible to seek justice in court if the school systematically refuses to provide a disabled child with the help he needs. Of course, one hopes that this will not be necessary. Understanding the law and insisting on its reasonable application is crucial.

Section 504 also protects ADHD adolescents from discrimination in school and in the workforce, at least in theory. However, it is incumbent upon the individual with the disability (or his or her parents) to inform the educating body and make reasonable requests that measures be taken to accommodate the student's special needs. Not all schools are as helpful as they should be, and students and parents are within their rights to insist on that the provisions required by law are actually provided.

Take charge of ADHD. Don't let ADHD take charge of you!

Bibliography

American Psychiatric Association *Diagnostic & Statistical Manual of Mental Disorders (DSM)* (4th Edition), (1994).

Barkley, Russel A., "Research Developments and Their Implications for Clinical Care of the ADHD Child", *Psychiatric Times*, July 1996 Vol. XIII Issue 7.

Cook, Maria, "Stop! Look! Listen!" *Ottawa Citizen Weekly*, December 9, 2001.

Gordon, Michael, *ADHD-Hyperactivity: A Consumer's Guide*, GSI Publications, 1990.

Gordon, Michael, *Jumpin' Johnny Get Back to Work!: A Child's Guide to ADHD/Hyperactivity*, Gsi Publishers, 1991.

Hippocrates, "Aphorisms", *The Genuine Works of Hippocrates* (Translated from Greek by Francis Adams), Krieger Publishing, 1972.

Hoffman, Heinrich, *The Story of Fidgety Phil*, Struwwelpeter, Feral House, 1999, (orig.1863).

Sonuga-Barke, E. et al, "Does maternal ADHD reduce the effectiveness of parent-training for preschool children's ADHD?" *Journal of the American Academy of Child and Adolescent Psychiatry*, 41, 2002 696-701.

Walker, H.M., and Walker, J.E., *Coping with non-Reliance in the Classroom: A Positive Approach for Teachers*, Austin, TX: Pro-Ed, Inc., 1991.